Wake Up & Dream

BECAUSE YOU CAN'T SEE THE FUTURE IF YOU'RE STILL ASLEEP!

BILL QUAIN, PH.D.

ACKNOWLEDGMENTS

I could never write a book like this without some serious help and inspiration. My thanks to the following people – your input is evident in this book.

My wife, Jeanne Quain – once again, Jeanne was there for all the "What do you think of this idea...?" discussions at breakfast, late at night, driving in the car, etc. Jeanne, you are tireless. Thanks so much.

Katherine Glover – Katherine, as always, you kept me going in the right direction. I can always count on you for some "real advice." Sometimes it sends me back to the drawing board, or to a major rewrite, but it always, always makes the book better. Many thanks.

Jack and Elizabeth Parry – No matter what the request, and no matter how short the deadline, Jack and Elizabeth have always delivered! This is at least my twentieth book with you two. I don't know how you do it, but thanks for doing it so well.

TABLE OF CONTENTS

Introduction – It's Ironic!

In 1993, I began to write my first "wealth – building" book. It was called *Reclaiming the American Dream: the keys to financial freedom*. One of the principles of that book was to create additional income. Like many authors, I defined additional income as "income that comes from non-job sources." This means, essentially, creating income through building a business. And, like many authors, I envisioned that the "right" kind of business would be able to generate that money "even when you are asleep."

But, after 25 years of writing books on additional income, wealth-building, personal growth, time poverty, and other topics, I can now concede that there is one great irony.

It is possible to *enjoy* additional, business-generated income – with money coming in while you are asleep. However, if you're going to *create* that kind of income, you must be awake when you do it. In fact, you must be Wide Awake!

And, that is the point of this book. *I want you to* Wake Up and get to work. If you want to create a lifetime of freedom – for yourself and your family – you need to be awake. If you want to build huge Dreams, you must be Wide Awake. If you want to find a business opportunity – a vehicle that will help you achieve your Dreams – you need to be Wide Awake. And, if you expect to be a great example to others, to people who really need your help, you must be Wide Awake when you do that as well.

In other words, you need to **Wake Up** and create a stream of additional, business-generated income, in order to be able to go to sleep and enjoy that money rolling in.

Wake Up and BUILD a Side Business

In 1993, most of us were writing about "breakthrough business building" that would allow you to completely break free from your current job or profession. Times change, however, and it is important to recognize that it is now possible to build a "side-hustle." Becoming successful today is not necessarily a "Choice A or Choice B" proposition. Your Dream doesn't have to be "to quit my job, and to live in luxury." Your Dream simply needs to be something that drives you to do something *out of the ordinary*, so that you can enjoy your life more fully. The concept is to *build* something outside of your job or profession. Some contemporary authors call it a "side hustle," or a "side business." But, in either case, it is a BUSINESS, and not just another job or some edition of your job. It is a business concept that has no boundaries, and no limits. You can build a business that DOES bring in money while you sleep. You can build a business that DOES replace some, or all of your current income. But, you can also build a business that simply gives you that extra "boost" of income, recognition, satisfaction and other rewards that really make life better!

Whatever kind of side-business you build, you can't do it without a strong, compelling Dream. And, you can't build a Dream if you are not wide awake.

Enjoy The Journey – but Get Going!

In my book *10 Rules to Break & 10 Rules to Make*, one of my favorite rules to make is *Enjoy the Journey*. Life is indeed a journey. Business-building and freedom-fighting are indeed journeys. But, you can't start a journey if you are asleep! *Starting* the journey requires decision-making. You need to develop a road map, set goals for various points of the journey, rally other travelers to go with you, etc. Most importantly, you need to be awake in case you need to make some changes in your journey. If you start a journey and go to sleep, you might end up anywhere!

A True "Start Your Journey While Sleeping" Story –
BIG MISTAKE!

In 1983, I was living in New Orleans, and dating my (future) wife Jeanne, who was living in Phoenix. Jeanne invited me to join her for a 10-day raft trip through the Grand Canyon. I booked an airline ticket from New Orleans to Phoenix, with a connecting flight in Dallas.

Everything went fine on the trip from New Orleans to Dallas, but *terribly* after that! In Dallas, I heard my flight called, and went up to the gate, where a flight attendant (called a "stewardess" in those days), looked at my boarding pass, and said, "Go right on sir." I found my seat, threw my carry-on bag in the compartment above me, sat down, and promptly fell asleep – before the plane even took off.

Now, you have to realize, this was a pre-9/11 era. It was a LOT easier to get on a plane in those days. Nobody was *really* looking, or being too careful. What I am about to tell you would not happen today.

I woke up while the plane was still in the air, but I did not know how long I had been asleep. I was dead-tired, because, like most of us, I did *everything* the night before an extended vacation. You know how it is. I was up late, catching up on all my work, packing, and cleaning the house. And remember, there were no cell phones back then. When you went away – you were really away, and would be out of touch with the office, friends, etc.

ANYWAY… the flight attendants announced that they wanted us to fill out a survey, and passed out the survey forms, along with some pencils. The first question on the survey was, "What is your flight number?" I wrote it down, because I always know my flight number. But, the woman next to me did not know the flight number, and asked the flight attendant what it was. The flight attendant gave her a DIFFERENT FLIGHT NUMBER than the one I wrote down! I began to get very nervous!

To Make a Long Story Just a Little Bit Shorter...

Yes, it was true. I was on the wrong flight. A few minutes later, the captain came over the loudspeaker, and announced that we would soon be landing in Midland Odessa. Now, at the time, I did not know that Midland Odessa was a city in rural Texas. In fact, I had never heard the name before, and I was wondering, "How long have I been asleep?" For all I knew, I was flying to some place in Alaska!

The good news was that I had left a day early for the raft trip through the Grand Canyon, so I was able to get on another plane, fly back to Dallas, and arrive in Phoenix late at night. But, I learned a valuable lesson: *If you are going on a journey, make sure you are awake!*

And, It's True for Almost Everything Important

Look, this story about my flight to Phoenix has a LOT of relevance for anyone who wants to have a successful life. If you want to make good choices, be there for opportunities, build relationships, and most importantly, avoid costly mistakes, you need to Wake Up and Stay Awake! When you are asleep – or even not paying attention – you can miss so much in life. And I am not just talking about being *sound asleep* – the kind of sleep where you lose consciousness. I am talking about the *mental lapses* we all go through, every day.

For example, what happens to you when you are watching television, or working on your computer, or looking at videos of dogs wearing funny hats on your phone? You might not be *technically* asleep, but no one would claim that you are Wide Awake!

The truth is, in these days of highly addictive technology, most of the world is asleep most of the time. Life is passing you by, and the people who ARE awake are taking advantage of your inability to focus and participate. They are feeding you reams of unedited, stupefying, *pabulum*, and you are sucking it down like the baby you have become, and then *really* going to sleep.

Wake Up America! Wake Up World!

That is the message of this book. You need to Wake Up and smell the money – or the relationships – or the opportunity – or the cries for help from the people you love! There is a whole world waiting out there, and all you have to do in order to be competitively ahead of almost 99.9% of the rest of the population is to Wake Up and do something constructive. You will be amazed at just how easy it is to get ahead if you do. And, if you take the time to Wake Up and take action, you will realize just how much you have been asleep.

This Is Your Alarm Clock

Okay, consider this: your alarm clock just went off! This is the start of your very first day as a Wide Awake individual. Make it a habit, and start Waking Up every day – ready to get to work.

Let's take our first step together, by going through this book, and beginning with your first challenge.

Wake Up and Dream.

CHAPTER 1

Control Your Dreams and Control Your Life

There are three kinds of Dreams. They are:

1. Sleeping Dreams
2. Day Dreams
3. Motivating Dreams

Everyone is familiar with the first two types of Dreams. Sleeping Dreams occur when you are… *asleep*. No surprise, right? You are tired, after a long day, and you drift off to sleep. Sometime during the night you start seeing a *video-like* set of images in your sleeping brain. Some Sleeping Dreams are vivid, some are muddled and fuzzy. Some make sense, others do not. Some are terrifying, some are peaceful. Some you remember in great detail, others are just dim memories.

But, all Sleeping Dreams have one thing in common – you have no control over them. You can't say to yourself, "I think I will have Dreams about… (whatever) tonight." It doesn't work that way. You Dream what you Dream when you are asleep, not what YOU want to Dream about.

However, you DO have control over your Day Dreams and your Motivational Dreams. You can turn them on or off, whatever you please. If you want to think about romance, go ahead. If you want to think about winning a race in the Olympics, be my guest. In your Day Dreams and Motivational Dreams, you can be, or do, whatever you want, for as long as you want. In other words, you have CONTROL over these two types of Dreams.

This is an important point, and I think it is worth spending some time on the subject. You see, while most people have both Sleeping Dreams (over which they have no control) and Day Dreams (over which they have full control), only a very few, very special people EVER spend time with Motivational Dreams. And that, my friends, is a real shame!

Asleep, Barely Awake, and Fully Awake Dreams

We will get to the subject of "being in control" of two types of your Dreams in a minute, but first, let's take a look at an interesting phenomena – just how sound asleep or Wide Awake you are when you experience each of the three Dream types – Sleeping Dreams, Day Dreams, or Motivational Dreams.

Most people will easily agree that Sleeping Dreams occur when you are asleep. No arguments, right? But, let me throw out a new thought. Your *Motivational Dreams* are the only Dreams you have while you are completely, Wide Awake. When you create strong, Motivational Dreams, you are active, conscious and alert. You are determining what *will* be – if you make changes and take action. However, with Day Dreams, you are in a much more passive state – in fact, you are often half (or more!) asleep. For most of us, Day Dreaming is just a way of taking off the pressure of everyday life. We aren't Dreaming about things we will ever take action to produce. In other words, while Day Dreaming, you aren't setting goals, nor saying to yourself, "I will make serious changes in my life, in order to make this Day Dream come true."

Day Dreams lull us into inaction, not action. We use Day Dreams to *substitute* for reality, not to *create it*. Look at the scale below, it shows how Wide Awake we are (or are not) when we are in any of the three Dream states – Sleeping, Day Dreaming, or Motivational Dreaming.

SOUND ASLEEP	DROWSY/ DISCONNECTED	WIDE AWAKE/ ALERT
Sleeping Dreams	Day Dreaming	Motivational Dreaming

Are You Getting This, or Are You Day Dreaming?

I teach college classes. My students have a very short attention span. They are always drifting off into Day Dreams, thinking about more pleasant subjects. It is not surprising that they have short attention spans – they are young (late teens, early twenties). Their entire lives are spent using technology, and that technology is separated into short, attention-grabbing bites.

However, even older people suffer from short attention spans. Let's face it, a lot of what we do in life is pretty boring. If you are working on a job, you can probably take a "few minutes off" from the routine things you are doing, and do a little Day Dreaming, right? If you are in a meeting, isn't it almost *impossible* to keep your mind on whatever is being said – no matter how hard you try? In fact, isn't it often *harder* to keep focused, the more you try? In just a few short minutes, you stop thinking about what is going on, and start thinking about how hard it is to stay focused! Pretty soon, it is ALL too difficult, and you simply slip away into a Day Dream!

But, let's face it. No matter when and where you Day Dream, you are almost always thinking about something more pleasant than what is going on around you, right? It is a form of escapism. Why pay attention to the math teacher, when you could be standing there on the winner's platform, getting your first (of many) Gold Medals! Why think about how to deal with a difficult colleague, when you could be swept off your feet by Prince (or Princess) Charming!

Day Dreaming Sells Lottery Tickets!

Why do people spend money on the lottery? They know the odds are stacked against them. Now, I have played the lottery all my adult

3

life. Why? Because I *Day Dream* about the things I could do with that money if I won. And, because it is a *Day Dream*, I am always a hero with the money when I win it.

For example, I am the oldest of 7 siblings. My wife has two siblings. We have two children, and lots of nieces and nephews. In my Day Dreams about winning the lottery, I invite everyone to our house, and then line them up and start giving out checks. (Well, actually, I *start* with cash, but soon, the amounts I am giving away become so large, that it makes more sense to give out checks.)

Here's how it goes:

We always start with my side of the family (I eventually give the same amount to Jeanne's side, but hey, that's *her* lottery Dream!). I go down the line, and give everyone $1. Then, I go back down the line, and give everyone $10. I keep doing this, multiplying the dollar amount by 10, until I finally give them all a check for $100,000. At this point, they have received a total of $111,111. I then explain that the $100,000 check was the real prize, and that the other money was so they could pay the 10% Gift Tax on all the other money. After paying the Gift Tax, each of them is left with $100,000 – free and clear. (Of course, I have no idea if the Gift Tax is actually 10%. It *used* to be 10% years ago, but remember, this is a *Day Dream* – I will deal with reality if I ever win the lottery.)

After giving everyone the money, they are all happy, excited, and most importantly, eternally grateful to me for my overwhelming generosity. (We are an Irish-American family, so there are many tears of course.) What a hero I am!

But wait, it seems there is just one more round. I ask them to tell me what the next amount will be if we keep the "10 times" sequence going. No one dares to answer. (My family is not good at math.) Finally, someone says it out loud. "Is it $1,000,000?" someone finally croaks out. And yes, it is! Jeanne and I hand out the final checks, and now each of my siblings has a check for $1,000,000 – and the money to pay the Gift Tax.

And, that's why I play the lottery! If I didn't have that Day Dream, I would never want to throw away $5/week for those tickets. It wouldn't be worth it.

The Irony of the Lottery

One thing always makes me laugh when talking to people about the lottery. I hear them say, "Wow, the lottery is up to $100 million this week, I think I'll play."

Are you kidding me? You wait until it is up to $100 million, and *then* you buy a ticket? What about when it is $1 million? Are you going to tell me that $1 million isn't more money than you will ever hold in your hand at one time? Are you crazy?

(A note from Bill Quain: The observation above, about people waiting to play the lottery until the money is astronomical, has nothing to do with this book. I just thought it was interesting!)

Playing the Lottery Is A Waste of Money, but...

Look, we all know that playing the lottery is a waste of money. Chances are excellent that you will never win. In fact, not winning is almost a sure thing! I can say with great confidence that no one who reads this book is going to win the lottery. After all, the chances that anyone who reads this book will actually win millions of dollars in the lottery is so remote, that my confidence level is extremely high.

But, I'll bet that almost everyone who is reading this book will play the lottery at some point. (My apologies to people who do not gamble for religious reasons.) Why? Why would people spend their hard-earned money on lottery tickets, even though they will never, ever win those millions of dollars? Simple – it is because of Day Dreaming. When you Day Dream, you always win! Have you ever heard of a *nightmare* Day Dream? No! Day Dreaming is powerful. It is also very, very dangerous. When we Day Dream, we replace reality with fantasy. We flee from reality. We escape to a world where everything goes well. It is addictive, and that is a real problem for many people.

Motivational Dreams – Wide Awake and Under Control

Let's review. We said there are three classifications of Dreams – Sleeping, Day Dreaming, and Motivating. You have no control over your Sleeping Dreams, but you do have control over your Day Dreams and Motivational Dreams. You are definitely asleep during your Sleeping Dreams, escaping reality (and semi-sleeping) during your Day Dreams, and Wide Awake for your Motivational Dreams. So, of the three classifications, which one of them is probably the one you want to spend your time on? Do you want to spend your time on Dreams you can't control (Sleeping)? Do you want to spend your time with Dreams that are simply an escape from reality (Day Dreams)? Or do you want to spend your valuable time on Dreams that will change your life in a positive way, forever (Motivational)?

Well… when we put it like that, there is really only one answer.

Obviously, you want to take full control of your life. You want to spend your time on things that matter. You want to be Wide Awake, and getting motivated to make positive changes.

Hey, play the lottery if you want. Escape every now and then. Get some sleep and get whatever Dreams come your way, but Wake Up – every day, and STAY AWAKE until you accomplish something positive – something that will create a lasting change for you and your family. Take control.

Get some sleep, but then Wake Up – and don't slip into Day Dreams. Oh, and one more thing, read the rest of this book!

CHAPTER 2

Wake Up, It Wasn't Just a Bad Dream

Warning: This chapter starts out badly. It is actually fairly grim! But, stay with me for a few pages, because there is some GREAT NEWS in this chapter. But first, I have to "stir your pain" a little, and then, the good news will seem even better!

I was speaking with a friend of mine this past week. This is a guy who works hard. He gets up early 5 days per week, gets dressed in a suit, and goes to a job he doesn't like very much. He works with people who aren't *bad* people, they just seem to have "blinders" on. Nobody really talks, or seems to be enjoying what they do. But, they all keep doing it, day after day, because of one fact – they all need the money! My friend has been doing this kind of job for years. He misses out on all kinds of events with his kids. He can't take time off from work to do something special with them, because he saves all his time to go on a vacation with the family once per year. He and his wife have a mortgage, two car payments, and some credit card debt. His oldest daughter just finished her freshman year in college, and my friend had to borrow a lot of money to pay for the tuition. He doesn't mind, because his daughter is taking on some of the debt herself. She will have to hit the ground running when she graduates, because like her father, she is going to have some hefty monthly payments to pay off the four years of borrowing.

Of course, there is one big difference between my friend and his daughter. His daughter only has her own college debt to pay off in the future. My friend has two more kids, and he will be taking on some of their debt as well.

What does my friend think about all this? He is willing to do it because he doesn't really have a choice. A mortgage, car payments (and those cars will only last another couple of years, and then he needs NEW cars), college loans and all the other debt will keep him working for a long time. His time just isn't his own. He goes to work because that's where the guy who pays him is. When that guy says, "Be at work today," my friend says, "Yes sir."

Last Week, He Had a Nightmare

When I met with my friend last week, he was telling me about a nightmare he suffered the night before. He said, "It was one of those Dreams where I was either running away from something or I was trying to catch something. I just can't remember which one it was. Anyway, I seemed to be stuck in some kind of mud or quicksand. I tried to run, but my feet just wouldn't move. It was so frustrating. The more I struggled, the worse it got. I just couldn't seem to get moving. Nothing I did was helping me."

"What happened?" I asked.

"I woke up," he said. When I realized it was just a nightmare, my first reaction was to feel relief. But then, I had a sickening feeling. It wasn't a nightmare. It was my life!"

I believe he was right. His life was a nightmare.

Asleep or Awake, What's the Difference?

In the previous chapter, we talked about the difference between being asleep and being awake. The BIG difference is that you have control over the things that happen when you are awake. When you are asleep, your mind Dreams. Images flash through your subconscious. You do not have any control over what you see, or feel.

When you are awake, you do have control – unless you give that control to someone else. When you incur debt, you put yourself into a situation where you are giving up control. Now, in order to get money to pay off that debt, you have to find someone who is willing to give you money. Of course, they want something in exchange. They want CONTROL!

If you Wake Up, and you find yourself out of control, or in the control of someone who does not have your best interests in mind, you are not really awake. You are asleep, and you are experiencing a 40 – 50 hour/week, continuous, unrelenting nightmare! You can't win. Asleep or awake, you are in the same position – all you can do is shut your eyes and hope the nightmare goes away. If you are really asleep, you might luck out. If you are awake – then you are out of luck, because the nightmare will continue as long as someone else is in control.

It Is Time To REALLY Wake Up

If you want to be successful, you need to Wake Up and take action. Don't put your life on hold by sleeping away your opportunities. The only thing that can happen then is that you will have uncontrolled Dreams and nightmares. And, don't spend your time in a "half-sleep" state, living in your Day Dreams instead of facing reality. You need to be Wide Awake, taking control of your time, your life, and your Dreams.

What is it like to be Wide Awake? You are living in the present, not the past. You have an eye on the future, but you are not procrastinating, stalling for time. You are taking charge of your life, and taking responsibility for your actions. And, your actions are made with full awareness and purpose, not out of a force of habit.

Think about my friend in the example above. He didn't start out his life thinking to himself, "I guess I will take a job, and borrow a lot of money, and just see what happens." He didn't say "I am not capable of creating income, and controlling my debt. I will just take a job with someone, and ask them to worry about all the details in my life. When I have kids, I will just pass on the bad habit of going through life, with a half-conscious awareness of what is going on around me. When I get really depressed, I will just take some time out, have some good Day

Dreams (where everything turns out right) and then face reality when my mind wanders back into the present. It will all be okay."

Maybe that isn't how my friend *started* his adult life, but it sure seems like he is living that way now – and chances are good his children will grow up and live that way sooner, rather than later.

What Do You Need to Do?

In this book, we are going to start with one, simple premise – Wake Up and Stay Up! Because when you are Wide Awake, you can do the following:

1. See opportunities as they present themselves (and they present themselves ALL THE TIME – but only if you see them!)

2. Avoid costly mistakes. Sometimes, it isn't a matter of going forward, it is also a matter of not getting stuck where you are now, or even worse, going backwards. Getting stuck or going backwards are much more likely if you are asleep, or half-asleep.

3. Meeting other, motivated people, and forming meaningful networks with them. Think about it. If you are a fully conscious human being – a person who wakes up and stays up for every day – you will be looking for other people just like you! It might take a while to spot them – among all the half-conscious people who are just, "Phoning it in." But, after just a short while, you will start to find the other people like you, who are awake and searching for answers that will set them free.

Folks, it isn't rocket science, and it isn't brain surgery. So, get ready. I am not going to ask you to do a lot. I am just going to ask you not to go back to sleep!

CHAPTER 3
Acting, Not Reacting

I want to show you how *antiquated* our ideas of human motivation are. For example, the most commonly accepted expert on Motivation today is Abraham Maslow. But, did you know that his work was published in 1943? He published a paper called "A Theory of Human Motivation" in *Psychology Review* 70 years ago – yet it is treated as the absolute truth today, and it is why YOU are now reading this book, because anyone who still thinks Maslow had it right is probably poor – or at least, in danger of going broke any day now!

So, when I say it is time to WAKE UP, I mean it is time to start looking at these commonly accepted beliefs with "Wide Awake" eyes!

Most people have heard about Maslow's Hierarchy of Needs. Maslow said that human beings solve their basic needs first, and then look for more "uplifting" needs. Maslow's Hierarchy of Needs is a pyramid shape. It looks like this:

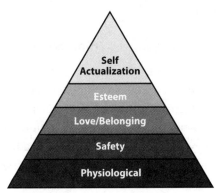

Colleges and universities all over the world, every class **on** motivation, management, sales or leadership starts with a discussion of Maslow's theories. It seems to be universally accepted. And, I'm not going to argue about it here. But, talking about a *Hierarchy of Needs* certainly doesn't have a lot of appeal when you are thinking about doing something different than the average person. You see folks, if you really want to get excited yourself, and if you really want to get *other people* excited, you have to go way beyond needs, you have to go all the way to DREAMS!

Maslow Is Looking Backwards

Let's think about this for a minute or two. Maslow is consumed with the idea that people will spend their time pursuing things (needs) they are already feeling. Well, *anyone* can do that! For example, Maslow says that people feel hunger, so they want to satisfy that hunger. So, they hunt for food (either the old way by going out and shooting it) or in the modern way (getting a job, so someone else will worry about the hunting). Do you see what I am saying here? Maslow says that human beings are *reactive* to their needs. He goes on to say that, once man has filled his basic, physical and biological needs, he will start to feel a need for something more. At this point, he might actually take steps to fill psychological needs – *but not until he feels those needs!* Finally, after getting almost all the way to the top of the pyramid, human beings start feeling a need for Self-Actualization. But, they don't pursue that need until they have done everything else, and all of a sudden that need is visible to them.

An Example of a "Backwards-Thinking" *Maslow Man*

Let's take a typical college student. (As a college professor, I see hundreds of these "typical" college students each year.) Now, almost none of them really face true physical needs. Every one of my students is getting enough to eat. Most of them can get food and shelter from their families if they need it. But, when they graduate, they do feel some basic needs for food and shelter, and so they take a job, because, even though they can get those things from their families, they are already starting to feel higher needs – like being more independent.

Why do these students want to be independent? Is it something they act on or something they react to? Let's face it, for most of them (and us) it is a reaction. What are they reacting to? Well, if they want to stay out late with their friends, or go someplace whenever they want to go, they simply have to get out of the house! If you are a young person, you know exactly what I am talking about. If you are an older person – especially an older person who has raised children – you also know exactly what I am talking about!

Now, let's say that "typical" young person is now getting a little older. Suppose she gets married, and has a child. Now, it is time to start thinking about a nicer home, more consistent living arrangements, and maybe a job that will allow her a little freedom. This is also reactive.

Finally, maybe the kids are grown, the house payments aren't so huge anymore, and a sudden urge comes over her to "achieve something in life." This is a good example of how Maslow's Hierarchy is reactive. At every stage, the person is reacting to needs they already noticed.

Maslow says "Great"!

When we study Maslow in college, this is EXACTLY what we learn – that people respond to felt needs. And, because Maslow is always talking about *already felt needs*, his solution to motivation is always based on reaction to those already felt needs.

This works very well if you are a *manager* or a *salesman*. All you have to do is to find someone with a need, and then fill it with some reward. That is why we work so hard for raises at work – but it is why we have to *continue* working so hard in order to keep that raise.

Rich Dad Poor Dad

In his breakthrough book *Rich Dad Poor Dad*, Robert Kiyosaki talks about the "treadmill." According to Kiyosaki, we work hard to get a raise, because we feel a need. But, when we get that raise, we don't save up the money in order to pay for the need (such as a shiny new car). Instead, we pay for the need (the car in this case) with a loan, or a credit card. Now, we not only have to work hard, we have to work even harder, in order to pay off the car loan – with all the interest. We filled a need reactively, and now we have to keep on working harder and harder, to pay for all the reactive payments!

This is how humans get trapped in our modern society. They simply *react* to their needs, and then do one thing to fill them – WORK on a JOB!

Unfortunately, this plan of feeling needs, reacting to that feeling, accepting pay from someone, and then having to work harder and harder (while piling up even more debt) is simply a no-win situation.

WHY IS IT A "NO-WIN SITUATION?

Let's go back to the Hierarchy of Needs. Take a look at it again.

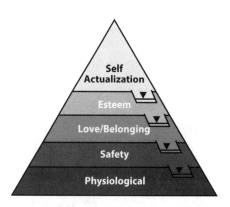

If you are always reacting to your needs, you will start to go to sleep! Think about it. If you are like the vast majority of people, you have only one way to react to felt needs - by taking wages on your job. You feel a need for food and shelter, so you take a job. You feel a need for even better food, and nicer, more impressive shelter, and you work harder - *on the same job*. Maybe, at some point, you take a better job, so you will get paid more. But let's face it, no one is giving you a better-paying job so you can enjoy your life more! They are giving you that better-paying job so you will work harder – for them.

But now you are feeling like an important executive, so you suddenly have more felt needs. "I can't invite people over to this home. I need a BIGGER home." I can't drive this car to work, I need a bigger, better, more expensive car." "I can't afford to pay cash for any of those things. I better take out more loans, or use a credit card." "Wow, those credit card debts are piling up. I better work harder."

Seriously now, do ANY of the statements above sound like you were awake when you made them? You simply did what everyone else around you did. You didn't think about it. You just did it.

If you had been Wide Awake, is it possible that you would have *looked ahead* instead of just *looking back* at your felt needs? Folks, if you REALLY want to reach the top of Maslow's Hierarchy, and become *self-actualized*, you need to Wake Up.

What Are Your Chances Of Becoming "Self-Actualized?"

Based on Maslow's theories, almost every psychologist and management professor today will define self-actualization as "personal growth towards self-fulfillment." It is probably a good thing that they describe self-actualization in such confusing terms, because I haven't seen many people out there who I would describe as "self-actualized", have you?

Here is a great way to gauge your chances of becoming self-actualized (if you can even figure out what it means). Take a look at all the people around you, who are basically like you. Do they appear to be self-actualized? Are they able to take their eyes off themselves, and start looking at the needs of others?

Sure, maybe you know men or women who are always busy volunteering for good causes. But, would you really consider them *self-actualized*? Don't they still have the same worries you do – not enough time or money to really relax and enjoy life? Are these people able to take off, whenever they want, to go on great vacations with their families? If they have an ailing parent, in another state, are they able to take off the time to go care for them? Are they so self-confident and assured that they do not get involved in petty grievances from time to time?

In other words, are they much different than you and me? Probably not.

Now, for the real acid test. Look around at the people you work with. Are any of them *self-actualized*? Is your BOSS self-actualized, or is she/he a nervous wreck about losing their job because you aren't working as hard as you need to work (in their minds)?

Folks, I have lived in several countries, and in several states. I had a lot of jobs, and have been hired as a speaker by numerous corporations and organizations. After all these years, and all those people, I can honestly say that I only met a handful of people that I would consider as *self-actualized*, and NONE of them were my bosses!

So, who are the self-actualized people I met? They are all wealthy. They all accomplished a great deal in their lives. And, each and every one of them was Wide Awake! Each and every one of them did something out of the ordinary. NONE of them were workers in a factory, or in an office, or a mid-level executive. A few of them were tradespeople – but every one of them had their own business. Only one of them was a professor (but he also owned several businesses). ALL of them were individuals who had chosen a different path for themselves. They were all happy and excited. Each of them looked forward to every single day.

Interestingly, ALL of them had sadness in their lives – just like the rest of us. NONE of them was wrapped up in a hopeless cause. ALL of them were realists.

Oh, and one more thing. Each of them had a Dream… a clear vision for what they wanted their lives to be, and what they wanted *other people's lives* to be.

And, every single one of the really cool people I have met were positive, forward-thinking, *non-reactionary* people.

They didn't look back on their needs, they looked forward – towards their Dreams!

Would You Like To Be Self-Actualized?

I am not seriously asking you this question. Because, really, no one really understands what *being self-actualized* is. It is just an academic term that people use because Maslow used it, and four or five generations of people have been trained to use the word.

But, I will ask you, "Would you like more out of life?" Would you like to get relief from the terrible stress you feel right now? Would you like to have time to go on vacations, and the money to make them real? Would you like to look ahead, and see something positive and special in your life?

Most of all, would you like to have some *control* over your life? Would you like to wrestle control away from a boss, or the bill collector, or the multitude of really crazy people who are making your life so stressful right now?

Okay, I can show you how to do that. I can show you how to make it happen. And, it isn't because I am so wonderful. It is because I was Wide Awake enough to recognize that some people really made a difference, and I studied what THEY did in their lives.

Here is the good news. NONE of the really special (okay, call them "self-actualized) people I know started out that way. They grew and changed. They built their success and they designed their lives. They didn't get trapped in the silly, meaningless arguments that most of us spend too much time on, and they didn't *accept* what was offered to them.

You can do it as well.

CHAPTER 4
The Look Back Trap

In the previous chapter, I pointed out how the Maslow Hierarchy of Needs pyramid was a backwards-looking system. You are always responding to the most pressing need *that already exists*. If you are hungry, you can't concentrate on anything but food. If you are lonely, you can't concentrate on anything but finding someone. It is what Maslow claims will MOTIVATE your behavior.

Of course, Maslow goes on to explain that you can move on to higher aspirations, but only after your more basic needs are met. And, for the most part, that is how American businesses operate. It is what is taught in schools of business as well. It is how most professors (and even business consultants) suggest that you motivate people.

For example, if you go to work for a company, you are trying (first) to make enough money for food, shelter, clothing, etc. If you have a really good job, with decent pay, and you LOSE that job, you are scrambling around, trying to find something that will keep your old lifestyle going. If your old job paid you $100,000 per year, you probably had a lifestyle that people who make that much money have. You have a nice house, with nice cars. You are going out to dine at nice restaurants, and you take nice vacations.

If you lose that job, you try IMMEDIATELY to find another one that pays as well. Maybe you don't find anything for the first month or so. What do you do then? You SCRAMBLE even more, right? After all, you have bills to pay.

Suppose, just before you lost that good job, you were saying to yourself, "Things are going well for me. But, I would really like to become a more open-minded individual, because I want to have better relationships with people. Maybe I will enroll in a self-help class to improve my ability to communicate with my co-workers."

Okay, that seemed like a great idea when you had all that money coming in, right? But, what are you thinking about that course now? It has been thirty days since you were laid off. You are running low on money, but the bills keep coming in. How important does "learning to communicate better with co-workers" sound now? Not so important, right?

Another 30 Days Pass, and Still No Job

Oh no! You certainly didn't have this in your plan, right? It is now two months since you were laid off. What do you get rid of next? You can't sell your cars. You can't sell your house. But wait, maybe there will be no family vacation this year.

And, Another 30 days

You can't even remember that plan to take a "communicate better with co-workers" class. Your mortgage payment is looking like a huge mountain! You don't really need that fancy house, but you can't sell it either – or at least, not quickly. You will now take almost ANY job, just to have money coming in. In fact, you take TWO jobs, because one job doesn't pay enough for the lifestyle that you put on credit.

Maslow's Pyramid Has Trap Doors on Every Level

Let's take one more look at Maslow's Pyramid. You probably didn't notice this before, but there are trap doors on every level.

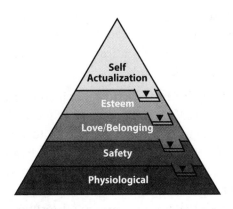

Here is the problem with Maslow, and why using a "looking back" system is no way to plan your life. You see, when you are responding to immediate and pressing needs, you are always in danger of falling back at least one level – at any time. Now, I'm not saying that this is not an appropriate way to act when an emergency arises, but it is no way to go through life! It means you are always just one misstep away from *emergency* mode. You can quickly fall from Self-actualization, down to Esteem. And, if the next crisis comes along, and you find yourself with a more pressing need, you can fall into the Love/Belonging level.

Again, I am NOT saying you shouldn't do this, but why would you think this is a good motivation system? If you believe in Maslow's theory of motivation, it means that you are *eternally* subject to the misfortunes that befall all of us during our lifetimes. And, if you are trying to motivate others, you are subject to every misfortune that occurs in THEIR lives. Do you really want that drama?

Wake Up, This Isn't NEWS

Look, here is the point I want you to understand. Life ALWAYS hands us challenges. It might be a change in health, or job status, or marital status. Bad things happen.

But, you know that! Don't you?

If we all know that bad things are going to happen, why would we possibly live with a system of motivation and inspiration that is ALWAYS going to be under attack from outside forces? How can you live like that?

Well… you wouldn't be living like that if you were Wide Awake! If you could only WAKE UP to the realities of life, and stop believing, and relying on a system that is absolutely filled with chaos and remorse, you might find life much easier to live. You might discover the peace of mind that comes from being prepared to live in a world that was never really designed for your comfort. If you Wake Up, you can make plans and create a lifestyle that is impervious to misfortunes.

As one of my friends says, "You want to become bullet-proof!"

Choose Your Dreams

Do you remember in the Introduction to this book, when we talked about the three categories of Dreams – Sleeping Dreams, Day Dreams and Motivational Dreams? If not, take a quick review, because this is important. Of the three Dream categories, which is the only one with the word "Motivational" in it? Easy – It is Motivational Dreams.

You see, Maslow got it completely wrong. He really did. And, generations of people have been taught to believe in something that is absolutely and completely NUTS! But, that is because so many people are asleep at the switch!

If you have Sleeping Dreams, but no Motivational Dreams, you have no control over your life. If you have Day Dreams, but not Motivational Dreams, you have no control in your life. Instead, you are either totally asleep (Sleeping Dreams) or unconscious (Day Dreams). You need to Wake Up and get ready for the crises you know are coming.

Motivational Dreams are Forward-Thinking

In the next chapter, I will be talking more about the kinds of Motivational Dreams you should be having, but for right now, let's just talk about why Motivational Dreams are so much better than Maslow's Needs.

Suppose you learn to build Motivational Dreams, and you choose a Dream about your lifestyle. In this Motivational Dream, you picture yourself living on the water, with a nice boat, and plenty of time to go fishing. In this Dream, you see yourself as relaxed and SECURE. This makes you a nicer person, because you do not have the stress or worry that comes from insecurity about money, or health, or other things. It is a great Dream. You spend a lot of time building the details. You write them down.

If you have a LIFESTYLE Dream, you have a great Dream. Lifestyle Dreams are fine. They are forward-looking. You are Dreaming about a WAY of life – without stress. It isn't just the *location of your home or the size of your boat*. Your LIFESTYLE Dream means you are secure.

So, how do you become secure? You plan for the calamities, and build your lifestyle slowly, with purpose. You have reserves. You do not overspend, putting yourself into debt. This reduces your risk. If there is some downturn, you have the money on hand to keep your lifestyle together, because you did not go into huge debt to attain that lifestyle. You *deferred gratification* until you had the money to pay for your lifestyle. And, you found a way to achieve your lifestyle by creating a business, or income that could continue to pay for your LIFESTYLE, even if you lost a job.

Do You Remember My Friends Who Were Self-Actualized?

In the last chapter, I told you that I met a number of people who were at peace. They were well-developed people, who had grown and changed enough to become better people – living a life of self-actualization. They were champions.

How did they get this way? They GREW that way. They built a life that was not dependent on credit cards and loans. They did not worry about losing their jobs, because they had built up ongoing income from their hard work and effort. When they got a raise on their job, they didn't immediately go out and incur debt, figuring they would pay for it with the raise. They were careful, cautious, but always growing.

You see folks, when you set forward-looking Dreams, instead of looking back at your last "need" and filling it as soon as possible, you can achieve great things. You can achieve peace of mind.

When you are forward-looking, you are Wide Awake. In fact, if you are like me, you had some kind of "wake-up call" that caused you to become a different person. That *wake-up call* caused you to change the way you do things.

Wake Up and Dream

Okay, that's enough about Maslow, and why you should look ahead at your Dreams, instead of looking back at your needs. In the next chapter, we will talk about your Wake Up call, and why you need to listen to it. It is the alarm clock that can turn your life around, and point you forward. It is your time to Wake Up. And, with the help of this book, and the help of people who love you and want you to succeed, you will learn to stay awake and prosper.

CHAPTER 5
Your Wake-Up Call

It isn't easy to suddenly Wake Up and Stay Awake. After all, most doctors agree that you need a solid 8 hours of sleep every night in order to function properly. If you DO sleep that long each night, you are spending one-third of your life asleep. That means, that for 33% of your life, you have no control whatsoever over your Dreams! Nightmares, confusing Dreams about people you love, angry Dreams about people you particularly DO NOT love – they can all come and go without you being able to do a single thing about it.

On the other hand, if you do not get 8 hours of sleep per night, you might not be Wide Awake during the day, and this will, again, cause you to lose control over your Dreams. You simply will not have the energy to create Wide Awake Dreams. If you are sleep-deprived, it is very difficult to focus on the future. You spend your energy just trying to get through the day.

We Need an Alarm Clock

For most of us, we need some kind of Alarm Clock every morning so we do not oversleep. I don't know about you, but I use my iPhone. I set it each night, and then, in the morning, it wakes me up. I set the alarm so that I will have enough time to do everything I need to do to get ready for the day. In other words, I PLAN my time so that I am Wide Awake in time to be effective when I go about my day. I want to make sure that there is a separation between my sleeping time, and my Wide Awake, productive time.

For example, I am writing this book on a Friday evening. Tomorrow morning, I am going fishing with some friends. We are leaving the dock at 6:30 a.m. I am going to set my alarm for 5:30. But, to make sure I will be in the car in time to stop off at a coffee shop, I already have my rods and tackle box laid out, as well as the clothes I am planning to wear, (and, of course, my safety gear, such as my inflatable life jacket.) I want to be Wide Awake when we hit the water.

I am sure you do the same thing, right? You make plans to get up at a certain time, and then prepare yourself for it. When you hear that alarm, you might not LIKE the sound of it, but it gets you moving, right?

What About Your Alarm For Building AWAKE Dreams?

Folks, almost all of us know exactly how to set a traditional alarm clock. But, few of us are equipped to set an alarm clock to help us Wake Up and see an opportunity, or recognize hazards, in our actual lives. The whole world is setting alarm clocks in order to get up and go to work, or to do other things, but almost NO ONE has set an alarm to go off when it is most important – to help us Wake Up and live our lives differently. Almost everyone is ready to Wake Up and go to their jobs – we are trained to do that. (And, going to your job is a good idea!) But almost none of us has set an alarm that will go off when someone – or something – alerts us to the fact that we have been virtually sleepwalking through life, never noticing that:

1. Things aren't going so well, and

2. There is an opportunity staring us in the face!

That Alarm Is Ringing All Around Us

Here is a VERY important point. The alarm bell should have been sounding all of your adult life. When you see friends get laid off – from the same kind of job you have – you should have heard the alarm. When your daughter was getting married, and you didn't have the money to give her a nice wedding, the alarm was ringing but you didn't hear it. When your brother-in-law, who is dead broke, warned you against an opportunity that you thought about taking, your alarm should have been ringing so loud that the bell should have broken!

On the other hand, when you saw people, just like you, who had financial freedom, and the ability and time to go where they want, when they want, your alarm should have been jumping off the table. When you see the car you have always wanted, being driven by someone who really doesn't look as smart as you are, your alarm should be shocking you like an electric current!

Folks, they call it an "ALARM" for a reason. It tells you to Wake Up. Start listening for it, and be prepared (just like I will be tomorrow when I get up to go fishing) and have all your stuff in order, so you can Wake Up and Stay Awake, and start living your life like it was intended you should live it! Be prepared. Be excited. Be Awake!

My Personal Alarm Clock Started Ringing on July 7, 1993

Yes, I know that 1993 was a long time ago. But, guess what? It was the day when my life changed, and the lives of my wife and daughters changed – forever. And, I can tell you the exact TIME it happened. It was at 2:30 in the afternoon. How can I be so certain? Because I always know what time woke me up!

At the time, Jeanne and I were living in Orlando, Florida. We liked Orlando a lot, but it had one thing missing – it wasn't on the ocean. We LOVE the ocean – or actually, any kind of water. We love to boat and fish. We love the beach. We love the water!

Whenever Jeanne and I went on vacation, we almost always went to the beach. When we came back to our lovely house in Orlando, we would say, "Someday, we want to live at the beach." Don't get me wrong. Orlando is a great city. We had a nice house with a pool. But, it wasn't WHERE OR HOW we wanted to live.

On July 7, 1993, at 2:30 in the afternoon, we were sitting at a dockside restaurant, in Fort Lauderdale, Florida. I had just given a talk for a large group of independent business owners at the Hyatt Hotel. The restaurant was across the intra-coastal waterway from the Hyatt.

It was a hot day, and the iced tea glasses had that "dew" on the outside of them. Jeanne and I were just finishing lunch. Jeanne was pregnant with our second daughter, and our older daughter was asleep in her stroller.

Suddenly, a large shadow fell across our table. I looked up to see a huge yacht slowly cruising by. I mean… this was a really LARGE yacht! On the back deck, there was a group of people, holding glasses of champagne, and laughing.

July 7, 1993, at 2:30 in the afternoon, and my alarm clock started ringing big time! I was jolted to my core, and believe me, I was WIDE AWAKE. Jeanne was in the same condition. Here we were, just where we loved being – on the water – and there were OTHER PEOPLE doing what we wanted to do – relax with friends on a large boat! "Hey," I thought. "That's MY Dream."

I remember turning to Jeanne and saying, "Jeanne, there is money in the world, and we need to get more of it. We should be the ones in that yacht. We should be the ones who live on the water, not just visit it."

And then, we both said, "Let's do something about it!"

July 7, 1993, at 2:30 in the afternoon. The alarm went off, and I woke up.

I Had Been Sleep Walking

A few years before that incident, I had another alarm. I woke up for a while, but then sort of went back to sleep. I guess you might say I hit the "snooze" button. Yes, I had *begun* to act differently. I had all the tools to do something about my situation. But, that "snooze" button kept letting me fool myself into thinking that I was really making progress.

You know what I mean with the "snooze" button, right? It gives you the *illusion* that you are getting some much needed sleep. Instead, the "snooze" button just postpones your life-changing energy release.

It lets you fool yourself into thinking that going back to sleep, instead of WAKING UP and starting to fill your destiny, is okay. It isn't!

Look, when you set the alarm the night before, you did it for a reason. You might not have wanted to Wake Up, but you were the one who set the alarm, so it must have meant that you *needed* to Wake Up. Okay, so maybe you are telling yourself that all along your plan was to give yourself a little extra time to actually Wake Up.

Folks, whether it is the actual alarm clock in your room, or the kind of alarm I heard on July 7, 1993, when you hear that alarm, don't go back to sleep!

My life changed on July 7, 1993, but it *should* have changed at least two years before that! I lost two years to my snooze alarm. Instead of watching that yacht from the dock, I might have been standing on the bow, wearing a stupid looking captain's hat and a blue blazer with white pants! But NOOOOOO, I hit the snooze button – for two years.

How Did Our Lives Change?

After hearing the alarm, on July 7, 1993, the first thing that Jeanne and I did was to start Dream-building. We were very specific about it. We found pictures of the things we wanted, cut them out of magazines, and put them on the refrigerator with magnets. We took a large piece of paper, wrote our *specific* goals and Dreams on it, and pinned it above my chest of drawers in the bedroom. Every night, before going to bed, I read my Dreams. Each morning, when I was getting ready for work, I read my Dreams.

5 years later, we bought a house on an island in Biscayne Bay, and a nice boat at our dock out back.

We raised our daughters to be boaters. We went fishing all the time. We took vacations with our boat. About 9 years later, while fishing in the "Big Fish" tournament in Miami Beach, our daughter won – by catching a large King Mackerel. With that win, she qualified for the Junior Angler World Championships. She finished 4th in the

World that year. Two years later, she repeated her Miami win, and the whole family joined her for her second World championships.

We took family vacations. We helped our parents. Jeanne stayed home with the kids. We traveled to many places where I was speaking. We had time. We had a LIFE that was much better than we would have had if I had not heard the alarm clock go off that day.

And, I didn't Snooze!

I just mentioned to you that I heard the alarm TWO YEARS before I finally woke up on July 7, 1993, at 2:30 in the afternoon. But, when I did hear it that day (you know the date by now!), I Woke Up and Stayed Awake. And, I shared with you the things that happened with our family – just because Jeanne and I Woke Up, Stayed Awake, and *did something about it*, after hearing that alarm (you know when!). But, what if I had hit the snooze alarm again? Would we have moved to the water? I doubt it. Would my daughter have won the Big Fish championship, and then finished fourth in the World? I doubt it. Would we as a family have had the time to travel, have fun together, and grow together? I doubt it. Would Jeanne have been able to stay home from work, FOR 19 YEARS as the children grew, went to high school, and then gone on to college? Definitely NOT.

Now look, you are probably younger than I am. In fact, you might be younger than I was in 1993. So, maybe you are thinking, "I have the time to wait. I can go back to sleep for a little while longer. It won't hurt anything."

Folks, if you are thinking that way, you are wrong – dead wrong. If you are lucky enough to have heard the alarm – the *right* alarm that tells you that your life is only just average, and average is a dangerous and frustrating way to live – then don't go back to sleep! Wake Up. Stay Up. Get Something DONE today!

Have You Hit The Snooze Button?

Look, let's be serious here. If you are the kind of person who is reading this book, you obviously experienced some kind of Wake

Up alarm, am I right? I mean, this isn't the kind of book that people randomly pick up. No, SOMETHING happened to you to make you read this book.

- Maybe you belong to a company that has a Book of the Month Program, and you got this book there. Okay, but what made you join that company? THAT was your alarm.

- Perhaps someone gave you this book, and said, "I think you will find this interesting. Get back to me if you think this book has a message for you." If that is the case, you are fortunate that someone thinks enough of you to help you Wake Up.

- On the other hand, you might have just reached the end of your rope, and you are seriously looking for something – *anything* – that will help ease the pain you are feeling!

It doesn't matter why, or how, you started reading this book. But now, you have two choices:

1. Hit the snooze alarm and go back to sleep, or
2. Let this book be the LAST Alarm you need to hear before changing your life forever.

It's Easier to Wake Up If Someone Else is Already Awake

Pretend this is Christmas morning, and you have young children in the house. You were up late last night, getting everything ready. Now, it's 6 a.m. and your kids are Wide Awake. Your alarm clock goes off, and just as you are about to hit the snooze button to get another ten minutes of much-needed sleep, the kids hear your alarm and shout something to you. What are they saying?

"Mom, Dad, it's Christmas Day. Santa was here. C'mon, get up. Wake Up. We're ready to go open our presents!"

(Yes, I realize that Christmas is about more than presents, but stay with me. Stay focused!)

With your kids dancing in the hallway, are you going to go back to sleep? Are you willing to hit that snooze alarm – even just once – and risk disappointing them? No, of course you won't.

Well …..

Maybe you are not reading this book on Christmas Day, but guess what? You just got a present – and it is in your hands! But, this isn't a shirt you will have to try on to see if it fits. It isn't a gift card – with a set amount of money in it.

This book is the kind of gift that keeps on giving – but only if you give it a chance to work for you.

Don't go back to sleep. Don't hit that snooze button. We are all awake and dancing in the hallway. We are ready to rush downstairs with you, and enjoy the wonderful day together.

Don't disappoint us. Get up and get going!

CHAPTER 6

S.M.I.L.E.S. – Your Wide Awake Dreams

Earlier in this book, I talked about Maslow's Hierarchy of Needs. Maslow says that people respond to needs, starting with the lowest level (Physiological Needs), and that a *few* people grow to the highest level of needs (Self-Actualization Needs). And, if you remember, I wrote about how Maslow didn't quite get it right. He tried to convince us that *needs* were big motivators. Unfortunately, there are two big problems with using *needs* as motivators:

1. You are always looking backwards, and
2. Each level of *needs* has a trap door in it. It is too easy to fall through the trap door and get stuck in lower-level needs.

Dreams Are Different

Don't be held captive by your *needs*. Instead, use *Dreams* to set yourself free! There is a huge difference. Dreams are forward-looking. Yes, you might slip a bit while working towards Dreams, but because you are always *looking forward*, you won't fall through the trap door and get stuck.

Look, life is tough, and you are going to have setbacks along the way to your success. There will be financial crises. You might have some health problems. People are going to discourage you from looking and acting differently. All these things are going to happen to you – without question. If you are always looking back, trying to satisfy the strongest need that is pressing on you at the moment, you can easily stop trying to make significant and lasting changes in your life. You will soon find yourself in the same position as everyone else around you – average, *at best!*

In this chapter, I am going to show you exactly why Dreaming is so much more powerful and positive that responding to needs. But first, let's look at a *different* hierarchy, a more positive hierarchy – S.M.I.L.E.S.

WHAT ARE S.M.I.L.E.S.?

S.M.I.L.E.S. are the six stages of Wide Awake Dreams that people go through on their way to a really powerful life. S.M.I.L.E.S. stands for

- Survival
- Material
- Income
- Lifestyle
- Expressive
- Spiritual

Here is a graphic that shows the hierarchy of these Wide Awake Dream Stages:

Spiritual
Expressive
Lifestyle
Income
Material
Survival

The Visual Differences between S.M.I.L.E.S. and Maslow

Let's look at the two hierarchies side-by-side.

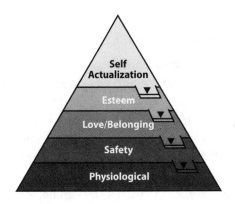

| Spiritual |
| Expressive |
| Lifestyle |
| Income |
| Material |
| Survival |

The first thing you will notice is that Maslow is a pyramid *shape*. This tells us something important. It tells us (and this is Maslow's Theory) that only a few people will become Self-Actualized. In fact, because Maslow basically says that people are always being pulled backwards by their most pressing, and lowest-level need, almost no one will actually make it to the Self-Actualized stage.

However, take a look at S.M.I.L.E.S. Each level is as wide as the one below it! EVERYONE has the possibility of reaching the Spiritual Stage of their Wide Awake Dreams. I mean it – _everyone and anyone_. It doesn't matter who you are, and how well off, or how un-well off you are, you can have reached your Spiritual Dreams while you are Wide Awake. There is nothing stopping you. Because unlike Maslow's Hierarchy, you are not responding to needs.

The second thing you will notice is that there are no trap doors in S.M.I.L.E.S. Remember, you are not responding to a *need*, you are looking ahead, at a *reward*. There is no "falling back and getting trapped" when you Dream, instead of responding to needs.

Here is what I am going to do for you in the next few pages. I am going to explain S.M.I.L.E.S., and then show you exactly why Dreaming (looking for rewards) is so much more powerful than *Needing* (responding to your urges). Sound fair? Okay, let's go!

You've Got S.M.I.L.E.S.

Okay, here are some thoughts on S.M.I.L.E.S.

<u>Survival Dreams</u> – These are your most basic Dreams. There is an old saying that goes, "If you are in the Survival stage, you are just trying to have as much *money as you have month*." Doesn't this make sense? Let's face it, most people in the world today are worried about simply surviving. They are working for a paycheck. They trade their time for dollars. Every month, they get the same amount of money for their work, and every month, they have bills they need to pay. Their bills include rent (or a mortgage), insurance, food, clothing, etc. They probably have a car payment, and they have to pay for utilities. All these things add up, and sometimes, they add up to more money than the wage earner brings in. This means they run out of money, before they run out of *MONTH*! This can be a real problem. Survival Dreams are the lowest order of Dreams. It is okay to have Survival Dreams.

<u>Material Dreams</u> – It is one thing to have a car payment that is just part of *surviving*, but let's face it, your *survival* car isn't going to be very motivating, is it? I mean, what kind of car are you driving if it's just something to get you around? That's why Material Dreams can be powerful motivators. With Material Dreams, you focus on getting *things* that really attract you. When my wife and I saw that yacht on July 7, 1993, at 2:30 in the afternoon, we WANTED A BOAT! A boat became my powerful, Material Dream. It is okay to want things. Jeanne and I cut out pictures of boats, and put them on our refrigerator. I looked at boats all the time – at boat dealers, marinas, etc. It was a great motivation to me. Now, you might be saying, "Who wants a boat?" No problem, owning a nice boat was my Material Dream. What's yours? (BTW, I often hear people say, "It is wrong to want Material things." If you are one of these people, stay tuned! We will cover this in the next chapter.)

<u>Income Dreams</u> – The third level of Wide Awake Dreams is the Income Dream. I often hear people say, "If I could just make another _____ dollars per month, I would be okay," or, "I need a raise,

because I want to live better/take off some pressure/buy a house/pay for college/etc." This is an Income Dream. Income Dreams are okay. In fact, they can be very motivating. But, make sure it is a) the right kind of income, and b) that you will put that income to the right use. I LOVE Income Dreams, because it demonstrates to me that the person who has an Income Dream is *motivated* to make more money, not just to cut back on their spending. This shows me that the person with that Income Dream is forward-looking.

Lifestyle Dreams – Okay, now we are talking! The first three Wide Awake Dream Stages are great – more people should be looking forward, but the first three stages are *lower-order* stages. Lifestyle Dreams are the first *higher-order* Dream Stage. Here is the definition of *lifestyle*. It is "Having money, and having the time to spend that money." Folks, this is powerful stuff. You need to develop Lifestyle Dreams in order to really get motivated. Imagine what your life would be like if the two biggest problems people face – not enough money & not enough time – were no problem at all to YOU and your family. This is BIG, BIG, BIG.

Expressive Dreams – Here is a question to ask yourself, "If you had all the things you need, and time & money were not a problem for you, how would you express yourself? In other words, what would you do that would make you unique, and let you make a statement about yourself? I asked two friends of mine this question. The first one said, "I love music and the arts, but I am not talented in those areas. To express myself, I would love to become a donor to the arts, and help set up scholarships for kids who want to study music or theater." The second one said, "I always wanted to help handicapped people. Wouldn't it be great to have the money and time to set up special homes for them, so they could live within the community?" (Writing about this now makes me feel bad, because my Expressive Dream was to learn to play the ukulele!) Expressive Dreams are powerful! How would YOU express yourself?

Spiritual Dreams – This is the highest level of Wide Awake Dreaming. I don't know what your spiritual beliefs are, but I can sum up mine in a simple statement – "Honor God by helping others." I want to do something special to make this world a better place. It is important to me. What about you? Are you living *spiritually*? Are you rising above the usual clutter of life's distractions, and becoming a spiritual person? And think about this, if you really want to help other people, aren't you going to need time and money in order to do it? If you want a REALLY powerful motivator, conquer the lower-level problems and challenges you have, and focus on the challenges and problems that are facing other people. Your "spirit" will rise. Finally, when thinking of Spiritual Dreams, think about the really big issues that keep people in fear, near-poverty and hopelessness. Go for the BIG IDEAS when setting your Spiritual Dreams. Build a life of Liberty and Freedom – for yourself and others.

And, That's S.M.I.L.E.S.

Okay, that's it. That's S.M.I.L.E.S. It is a hierarchy, yes, but not an exclusive one. By that I mean that you do not necessarily have to complete one level of achievement before moving on. Yes, it is sometimes difficult to get someone to focus on a sense of personal financial freedom, when their home is about to be repossessed. On the other hand, if you are going to work with someone, you wouldn't want them to be constantly fearing that they cannot pay their mortgage. You want them to at least begin to look beyond their present circumstances.

CHAPTER 7
Fulfill Your Destiny, Not Just Your Needs

A young couple was invited to a business meeting, to see an opportunity that some of their friends were promoting. The young couple really wanted to go, but their car did not have enough gas. "Let's put off that meeting," said the young man. "We need gas for the car, and until we get the money for that, we can't do anything else."

Here is a couple that is stuck in the present. They are stuck in the present because they are a slave to their *needs*, instead of being devoted to their destiny. They are, in fact, acting just like Maslow predicted they would act. They are acting like almost everyone else who is just like them. Their friends and family are all average, and this couple is the exact *average of those average people*. They are doing just what you would expect them to do – focus on short term needs, instead of facing the future with hope, and a desire to make a change, to make a difference.

Now, this couple was just DAY DREAMING last week about having more fun in their lives. They were DAY DREAMING about winning the lottery, and making some BIG changes – buying a new car, moving to a better neighborhood, sending the kids to college, taking more vacations, and having more time for each other. Pretty good DAY DREAMS, but nothing that would motivate them to make any changes (except, possibly, to spend more money on lottery tickets!).

Are you like this couple? Do you know people who are like this couple? They *seem* to want more out of life, but they just can't get past the fact that they aren't filling basic needs, and so they immediately fall back on the ideas and actions that are trapping them where they are.

What this couple does not realize is that they have a much more important need than filling the gas tank. They have a need for a Wide Awake Dream. They have a need for a new sense of Destiny.

It Isn't Just A Problem for People Who Are So Broke They Can't Pay For Gas

The couple mentioned above – without enough money to buy gas – isn't the only kind of couple with "Day Dream vs. Wide Awake Dream" problems. You see, *people are broke at all different levels!* And, it might not just be a matter of money that is holding them back. It could be that other great problem area – time!

Consider a different couple. This couple is a little older. They are both professionals. They have a beautiful home, VERY nice cars, plenty of money set aside for the kids' college education, etc. But, do you know what this couple does not have? They do not have TIME! Their professions – which pay a lot of money to them in salary – are also extremely demanding. It is not unusual for each of them to put in 50+ hours per week, and sometimes more. Both of them travel – but for their jobs, not for pleasure. Unfortunately, neither of them can take the time off from their work to accompany the other on a trip to a nice city, or a relaxing vacation.

When this couple heard about an opportunity, they said, "No way. We can't take on one more thing. We are just too busy to even *think* about doing something to break this cycle."

But, just like the first couple, the professional couple was just doing a bit of Day Dreaming. In fact, they also bought lottery tickets – because they fantasize about "having enough money to just quit and relax." Nice Day Dream, but it gets the people who do not win the lottery nowhere!

The Problem Is Needs vs. Destiny

In both cases above, these couples are reacting to felt needs, instead of developing a sense of destiny. It is really a question of maturity. When you were a child, you had no concept of the future. All you knew is that you wanted some things, and you wanted them now. If you didn't get them, you started crying, or throwing a fit of anger.

As you get older, you probably stopped crying, but you are still reacting to felt needs, and doing everything you can to address them, as fast as you can.

Look, I am not saying that you should absolutely not address felt needs. But, do it maturely! For the first couple, they obviously have some serious financial problems. So, they try to solve them by doing MORE of what they are already doing, because doing what they are already doing has worked out – at least for now. So, if they need more money RIGHT NOW to fill up their cars with gas, they might try taking on a second job, or selling something on eBay. That will bring them some short-term relief.

The professional couple is also acting immaturely. They have a time problem. So, they refuse to do anything except continue working on their professional lives. They keep thinking, "I need to get this work done, because we need the money to support our lifestyle. But, someday I will be able to cut back on this workload."

Well, *someday* isn't a real date. It is an excuse to keep on doing what you have always been doing, because it fills at least ONE need right now – money. But, it does nothing to actually give this couple what they really need – more time.

On the other hand, suppose both of these couples stopped focusing on the present and past – filling short term needs. Suppose they threw out all the misinformation they have been believing all these years – namely: get a good job, work hard, and save your money, because *someday* you will be all right.

You see folks, it is the belief in *someday* that is so dangerous, because by believing in *someday*, you are able to give yourself the excuse to focus on the short-term, need-fulfilling behavior that you (and everyone else like you) has been doing for so many years. Someday will kill you!

What you need to do is to stop thinking in terms of someday, and start thinking in terms of a *specific day*. *Someday* will never get here, but a *specific day* will ALWAYS get here.

WHEN MY WIFE AND I DEFINED A SPECIFIC DAY

When Jeanne was pregnant with our oldest daughter, her doctor told her that she would need to go on bed rest, in order to save the pregnancy. At the time, Jeanne was an Occupational Therapist, making a good amount of money. We had planned for her to stop working after the baby was born, but now, we had to face the fact that Jeanne would stop work TODAY! The problem was that we had not spent enough time arranging our finances to handle an *immediate* stop to her income.

We had a decision to make. We talked about it for some time. I could either take on a second job of some sort, or I could develop something that would create both income and time. In the first case, we would be responding to a felt need. In the second case, we would be designing our destiny.

Thankfully, we chose to design our destinies. Yes, in the short term, we cut back seriously on our expenditures. I also looked for some short-term cash solutions. But, we felt that we had a higher calling than to just "create cash flow." We wanted to create a lifestyle. And, that lifestyle did not include Jeanne going back to work.

For example, we could have said, "Well, even though we wanted Jeanne to stay home after the baby was born, we realize now that this is impossible. We are going to need the money. So, 6 weeks after the baby's birth, Jeanne can go back to work and we will use Day Care for our child." (Please note: I am not saying that staying home with the baby is right for everyone. It was what we wanted. Everyone needs to make their own decisions.)

What did we do? Luckily, we had a DREAM! Our DREAM was not rooted in a sense of felt-needs. We didn't make our plans based on the fact that we knew we were going to be short on money. We made our plans to fulfill the destiny that we wanted to create.

I *immediately* started looking at business opportunities. While I did several things, none of them had quick rewards. None of them were quick-fixes to our problem. But, ALL of them fit our Wide-Awake Dreams. EACH of them would bring in both money and time. I went to work right away. I didn't waste a minute.

In the end, we certainly had to tighten our belts for a while. It was a real shock to our financial system when we lost Jeanne's paycheck! But, eventually, my other businesses began to supplement my salary from my job. It meant working a lot of crazy hours – driving hard to build a business so that, in time, we would be okay. But, every bit of it was worth it. Jeanne stayed home for 20 years while our children were growing up.

Are You Convinced?

Okay, we spent a LOT of time talking about the difference between a Maslow*esque* approach to life – looking backwards, and responding to the most pressing need. And, we certainly covered the theme of looking ahead, with a Wide Awake Dream. Allow me to add just one more thought, and then we are going to turn the page, start the next chapter, and get you on your way to a forward-looking, Dream-fulfilling lifestyle.

In the end, I am not here to try to *prove* anything to you. I am simply laying out some thoughts to provoke you into an examination of your situation. Have I opened your eyes to the truth about the way *average* people think about their problems? That's the most important thing I can do for you with this book.

But, I promised one more thought, so here it is:

A shockingly high percentage of the people who win the lottery are broke again within five years.

How is that for a thought? Are you saying, "Bill, what does this have to do with me? I haven't won the lottery. Why are you wasting my time with this stuff?"

Folks, you DID win the lottery! But, you won a different kind of lottery. You are reading this book because *something* happened in your life. Maybe you had a financial crisis. Perhaps a friend said to you, "I want more out of life. I think I found a way to get it. Want to see what I am doing?"

It doesn't matter WHAT happened, but you won the lottery, because you have been given a chance to change your life. You now have the opportunity to get EXACTLY what you want in life. It is just like winning the lottery!

"But Bill," you are screaming at me by now, "Are you crazy? If I won the lottery, I would have MILLIONS of dollars in my pocket right now. My troubles would be over – forever!"

Well, chances are good that you would have MILLIONS of dollars for a while, but they are also VERY HIGH that you would be flat broke before five years had gone by! How can I say this with confidence? Just read the newspaper, or listen to the news. People who win the lottery do CRAZY things with their money. For one thing, every relative and friend that you ever had is going to show up on your doorstep, asking for money. It might be for an investment, or a loan, but they will definitely be there, with their hands out. WHY, because your friends and relatives know you did not WORK for that money. They know that you have no idea about what to do with all that money, so they figure, "Well, Bill just won that money. He should share it with his old cousin. In fact, I have been looking for just the right person to invest in …. (whatever!")

Not Having Money Isn't the Problem

Look, it turns out that not having enough money really wasn't the problem for the people who won the lottery, and then went broke. Their problem was that they had no idea what to do with the money once they had it!

Let's look at this a little more closely. Let's say you won a REALLY BIG lottery drawing – say $200 MILLION. First of all, do you know how to even handle that much money? I mean, think about it. It is $200 MILLION! Look in your bank account right now. Do you even have $200 THOUSAND there right now? Of course you don't. Some of us might not even have $200 in our account!

Now, of course, there are taxes to pay, and you may get the money all at once, or over twenty years. Both of these things are going to affect how much money you have on hand after winning the lottery. But, let's say you take a lump sum payout. You have to set aside taxes, so let's take out that money as well. Let's say, after the lump sum payout, and taxes, you receive $60 MILLION – in one, very big, check. (Okay, stop Day Dreaming, and get back to reading.)

Has ANYTHING in your life prepared you for what to do with $60 MILLION? Did you have a course on "What to do with $60 MILLION" in college? Have you read a book, with step-by-step instructions on what to do with this money? Do you even have a single friend or relative who can give you advice (THAT YOU WOULD FOLLOW) if you won $60 MILLION?

Let's face facts:

1. You have been working for someone else for years

2. No one in your family, or circle of friends, is really wealthy

3. The day after you win the lottery, you can quit work, but every other person you know in life is still going back to that 9 – 5, 50 weeks/year GRIND tomorrow. Do they want to hear about your problems – NO – especially if your problem is, "Cousin Eddie, what do I do with all this money?"

4. You can't just call up other lottery winners and see if THEY will help you. First of all, how are you going to find them, and second, THEY are struggling with the same question, and many of them have another question – "What happened to all those millions I won?"

THAT'S why so many lottery winners go broke within 5 years. They have no idea whatsoever about handling money – whether it is $60 MILLION, or $60!

But, You Won a *Different Lottery*

In the paragraphs above, I told you that you won a lottery when you bought (and read) this book. Look, SOMEONE recommended this book to you, right? You are reading this book because you are Wide Awake, and LOOKING for something that will change your life. You aren't just going to WIN the money you will make when you change your life. You are going to EARN that money. It is going to take some time, and most importantly, you're going to follow in the footsteps of other people who earned money. You just have to do what they did. And, when you start making money, you can do what they did to HANDLE that money and success.

That's why your lottery win is different. You didn't win the MONEY, you won the ABILITY to MAKE MONEY – whenever you need it. That's huge!

But, It Requires a Wide Awake Dream

I hate to go back to the "Maslow is a drag" argument, but please let me take just another stab at this, because it is SOOOO important to you. Remember, Maslow says, "fill your most pressing need – that is motivating." Well, because of your motivation from filling your most pressing need, you are stuck in a job, almost broke, in credit card debt, have a mortgage, and you are unable to do what you really want in life. But, if you build a Dream first, and then build a fortune, you are going on a journey of change and discovery. You are going to need to associate with positive, successful, caring people who will help you every step of the way. You will build a network of friends and advisors, *and all of those friends and advisors will be people who have already done the hard work, and who already have MONEY. They don't need your money. They need you to be successful!*

SHOCKING FACT: *If You Are A Maslow Believer, And You Win The Lottery, The People Who Show Up At Your Door Are Need-Fillers. If You Win the Lottery by Changing and Building, The People Who Show up at Your Door are Positive, Dream-Fulfilling People Who Don't Need Your Money.*

Here's what might happen:

Day 1 – You win the lottery - $60 MILLION is now in your bank account

Later in Day 1 – Every person in your PAST starts calling, emailing, showing up, and some even want to move in!

Day 2 – You are already on your way to being broke!

Now, contrast that with designing your destiny:

Day 1 – Something happens. Your alarm goes off. You suddenly realize that you are going nowhere!

Day 2 – You learn about an opportunity. (Maybe that was the alarm!!??) Someone cares enough to share their opportunity with you.

Day 3 – You think, "Well, that will never work for me. I better just go back to work."

Day 4- But, you can't shake the feeling that you can actually DO something about your problems. In fact, you start looking BEYOND your current circumstances, and Dream-Build your future.

Day 5 – You ask for help.

Day 6 – For the first time in your life, a successful person helps you.

Day 30 – Oh no. This isn't as easy as you thought it would be. Why do all your friends and relatives want to discourage you? (Hint: they don't want you to make money by doing something different, challenging, and forward-thinking. They wanted you to WIN the money, so they could ask for it.)

Day 60 – You are starting to associate with SUCCESSFUL people! What a difference. These successful people want YOU to be successful!

Day 120 – Wait! Did you just pay off a credit card? When did THAT ever happen?

And so on…

Folks, here is the difference between winning the lottery in a drawing, and winning the lottery through a great book, or an opportunity, or through a network of successful people. Are you ready to learn what is different?

Okay, let's make it simple. YOU are different.

You see, if you win the lottery in a drawing. The money changes you. If you win the lottery and it brings you opportunity, you change first, and then you get the money!

Why do so many lottery winners go broke? Mostly because they were broke when they won the money, and the reasons they were broke (or nearly broke) were bad habits, bad decisions, and bad associations! Now, you suddenly add a couple of million dollars into that mix of "badness," and you aren't going to have a good, long-lasting, positive, *Dream-Fulfilling* result. Truthfully, the real problem with winning MILLIONS of dollars, without changing your life first, is that you were *half asleep* when you won that money! That money was the answer to a *Day Dream*, not a *Motivational Dream*. When you are Day Dreaming, you are not fully awake. The alarm did not go off, and force you to change. So, there you are, operating in a half-awake, half-asleep mode, when PLOP, millions of dollars drop into your lap.

No alarm goes off. No buzzer is sounding a warning. Nothing is saying, "Hey, Wake Up. You have a problem here. You need to change, because if you don't change, you are going to lose all this money."

On the other hand, if you START with a Dream, and then build a life that helps you achieve that Dream, you are Wide Awake. Something woke you up. And, if you have a solid, forceful and inspiring Motivational Dream, it is quite possible that the alarm that went off was telling you, "Hey, if you are really serious about achieving this Dream, you need to make some BIG changes in your life. Look around you. Is *anyone* who is presently an important figure in your life capable of achieving the Dream you set for yourself?"

Folks, that was what set off the alarm for me on July 7, 1993, at 2:30 in the afternoon! I *wanted* something, and when I thought about it, nothing I was doing at that time, and *nobody* I was associating with at that time, was going to help me achieve that Dream.

I heard a MASSIVE alarm, and believe me, when that alarm went off, I was Wide Awake – and because of my Dream – and how intense it was – I *stayed* Wide Awake.

Phew, these last few pages wore me out! But, I am not going to sleep. I am not even going to take a break and go into a half-sleep. I am staying right with this book, because I want to help you find the right circumstances, the right words, or the right point of view so that YOUR alarm goes off right now, and keeps you Wide Awake until you realize your Dreams, and attain your true destiny.

Wake Up and Understand the Problem

Your problem isn't that you don't have enough money, or time, right now. Your problem is that you are looking backwards, letting every strong need dictate the terms of your life. You believed it when "they" told you to "get a good education, get a good job, work hard, and try to save as much as you can." You believed your boss when she told you that "working hard would lead to a promotion, and you will get a raise so your troubles will be over."

Why is that a bad statement from your boss? Because it turned out that she got fired six months later, and now nobody remembers what she saw in you! You are just another cog in the wheel, and you better do whatever cogs do – and keep on doing it – without complaining, because "We aren't so sure what a cog does either, and maybe we can get along with one less cog around here!"

Folks, your problems aren't in the past. They aren't in the present. Your problems are in the future. And, your solutions are in the future as well. You need a clear, STRONG vision of what your future will be like. You need a clear, STRONG decision about your future, and you needed it yesterday!

But, today will do just fine!

Do you want that new car or boat? Do you want a nice home – with no mortgage? Do you want to be able to take vacations whenever you want, for as long as you want? Do you want to make the world a better place? Do you want to express yourself in new and fulfilling ways? Do you want to become the strong, reliable, determined, generous, GOOD EXAMPLE of a human being that God intended for you to be?

If you DO want these things my friends, you are not going to achieve them by responding to every need, whim, desire and complaint that rules your life right now. If you give in to them, you will spend a lifetime as a slave to them.

No, be strong. Get a big, WIDE AWAKE Dream that drives your life and every decision you make in that life – until you have the life you want and deserve!

Keep reading. Your Destiny is Calling!

CHAPTER 8
Wake Up the Elephant

In this chapter, I am going to give you one of the most valuable lessons you will ever receive. I remember when I first heard about it. It really rocked my world! I had always thought of myself as a "free-thinking" man – able to make my own decisions, not held back by others. Wow, was I wrong! It turns out that almost all of us are held back by nearly-invisible bonds. We don't even notice them!

But, there is an even bigger benefit from the example I am about to give you. The example is so strong, that you can use it when talking to others. This is a HUGE benefit to you, because if you hope to Wake Up and become successful, you need to Wake Up others as well.

So, let's get right to it!

What Keeps Elephants From Running Away?

When I was young, I went to see the circus. There was a group of HUGE elephants standing around in a field, right next to the circus tents. Each of the elephants had a bracelet around one leg, and the bracelet had a thin chain attached to it. The other end of the thin chain was tied to a *surprisingly* small stake that had been hammered into the ground. The elephants were separated from the spectators by a *very* small fence! I watched those elephants for at least ten minutes. None of them moved. None of them pulled against the stake. None of them ran at the tiny fence. They all just stood there, rocking back and forth slightly.

Periodically, elephant handlers would come by and put water buckets within reach of the elephants' long noses. From time to time, other handlers would bring hay and put it in front of the elephants so they could eat.

Although I came back to the field of elephants several times that day, I NEVER saw even one of those huge beasts go and *get* hay and water. Instead, they waited and swayed, waited and swayed. I am sure they were either hungry or thirsty at some point, but they always waited for the water and hay to be brought within reach.

Even as a youngster, I realized that the chain and stake were no match for the elephants' strength. Any of those large elephants would find it no problem to either snap the chain, or pull up the stake. It just didn't make sense.

However, I DID see some baby elephants standing among the herd. For them, the chains really were a "tether" that kept them in place. For them, the chain seemed much larger, because it was strapped to a much smaller animal. For those baby elephants, there was no chance of moving around, even if they wanted to do it. They really were "chained to the spot" where they stood.

Of course, the trainers and handlers also brought food and water to the baby elephants. Those elephants got all the food and water they wanted. All they had to do was stand there, and everything they needed would show up for them – and would be easily in reach.

Did The Elephants Ever Get Off The Chains?

Now, let me tell you that I did not actually SEE those elephants being taken off their chains and stakes, but I do know what happened during the day – especially if the circus was either setting up or breaking down those huge tents.

When those enormous tents needed to be set up, the elephants were unhooked from their chains, and put to work. They would drag the tent poles out to the site, and then pull on them to lift them up straight. When the tents were being broken down so the circus could move, those same elephants would be unhooked again, and led to the work. There, they would be the main engines that provided the strength

But, That Wasn't the REALLY Surprising Part

It was shocking enough that the huge animals could be contained so securely by that thin chain and that tiny stake. But, think about the REAL surprise – a human being would take them off the chains, and walk them over to do the hard work. Can you imagine that? That enormous elephant would calmly walk along, under the direction of a human being that was maybe one *twentieth* the size of the elephant! And even more incredibly, whenever the human gave an order, the elephant just did what she/he was told – by this puny animal called a human!

How Does This Happen?

Let's take a crash course in "elephant training 101." As soon as an elephant baby is old enough, it is given a solid ban to wear around one leg. This band is attached to a chain, and that chain is driven into the ground. There is no way that small elephant can pull out that stake, let alone snap the chain.

Maybe the baby elephant gives it a try a few times. But, it *hurts* to pull on that chain!

On the other hand, that baby elephant looks around, and sees all the other *adult* elephants calmly standing there, NOT pulling on the chain. What does that baby elephant think? He thinks, "Well, it looks like I am *supposed* to stand here calmly. All the others are doing it."

And then, someone shows up with food and water. "Okay, that's good," the baby elephant is thinking. "I see that this is how we get all that good food and water. YUMMMM!"

Remember, Elephants Are Herd Animals

Elephants belong in herds of other elephants. That is their way.

It is ingrained in their minds. When they are born, the first thing they see is a large, mother elephant. That is food, and security, and *belonging*. There is security in the herd. If something goes wrong, or if the elephants are threatened, the bigger elephants gather around the babies and protect them. Being part of a herd is good. It is safe!

Being Chained Up Seems Better Than Being In the Middle Of Nowhere, with Lions, Tigers, Drought and Floods

Now, these tame elephants can't remember the days when their grandparents and great grandparents roamed around free in Africa and India. But, if they COULD remember, they would say, "Well... I sure hate being chained up to this stake, but it beats trying to find water when it hasn't rained for four months – especially with every hungry and nasty old lion waiting for me at the watering hole, not to mention those HUGE crocodiles that would LOVE to grab on to my nose when I stick it into the water. Yes, having a chain is a drag, but being dragged into muddy water by a crocodile who is biting your nose off is even worse."

Folks, in the wild, elephants would have to spend their entire day walking around, looking for food and water. If they get chained up, they get ROOM SERVICE – with the food being delivered to them.

But, It Isn't The Room Service That Keeps Them Chained!

Okay, let's go back to the baby elephants, who are chained up with bonds that are indeed strong enough to keep them there. These baby elephants become *conditioned* to the chains. They become *conditioned* to just standing around.

Later, when they are big enough to snap those chains, or pull up the stakes, they are already *conditioned* to the life of just standing around, waiting to be fed and watered. It doesn't even occur to them that they could break those chains. It doesn't even occur to them to pull up the stakes, and walk over to where all the food and water are being kept. They can't even imagine it! They really aren't even AWAKE!

Elephants Are Not Very Smart, Are They?

Hey, we are humans. We are the ones who figured out how to tame the wild elephants, so they would do our bidding. We figured out just how LITTLE it takes to keep those elephants docile, calm, and pliant. We are the ones who mastered those huge beasts – not with brute strength, but with our brains!

And, in fact, it was so successful, that some really smart human beings figured out a way to tame the *wildest and most dangerous* animal of them all – other humans! It was quite simple:

"Train them while they are young, surround them with others, and give them something basic – from Maslow's Hierarchy of Needs!"

Guess What? It *really* works!

The main point is to keep the other humans thinking about *needs* – and then filling those needs as inexpensively as possible. Even more importantly, don't let the other humans *Dream*! That is when they will realize that there are really no chains holding them, and that will be BAD for the humans who want us all to work, without question, and without let up. The LAST thing they want is for us to Wake Up and Dream!

Are You An Elephant?

What about you? Have you been chained up all this time, without realizing that all you have to do is pull out that stake and start *living*? Have you grown so accustomed to watching everyone else standing around, just like you, that you are afraid of losing the food and water ration that you are on?

Folks, it is an amazing story – the taming of the human race to go to sleep, or at least, sleep walk through the day, without ever looking ahead and seeing a different outcome. We have become so accustomed to trying to fill our basic needs that we never take the time to Dream anymore.

I Am Not Going To Tell You To Break The Chain or Pull Up the Stake!

Right now, you might be expecting to read these words:

"My fellow humans, be strong. Break those chains by using your God-given strength. Pull up those stakes and be FREE!"

Wouldn't that seem reasonable? Well… It is completely *unreasonable*! Here is why:

Those chains and stakes do not exist! How can I tell you to pull them up when they are not even there? Instead, just look down at your leg and see for yourself! Those chains and stakes are not on your legs, they are *in your minds*!

Get Out of the Herd (Mentality)

Is your herd holding you back? Are they all just standing there, waiting for their basic needs to be filled? Are they content to do the same work, day after day, in exchange for the most meager rations? Do they trade security for their FREEDOM? Do they stand calmly by, while others pursue their Dreams?

Folks, you know what the herd mentality 'is' right? In the herd mentality, no one in the herd does anything differently than anyone else in the herd.

Watch one of those nature shows on television. Did you ever see a herd get "spooked?" Something happens, and the entire bunch starts up all at once, and starts running. If they come to a cliff, many of them run right off!

In a herd, animals who do things that the others are not doing get pushed out of the herd. Now they are alone. That isn't good for a herd animal. It is frightening. That is why animals who are in a herd do everything they can to stay in the herd.

Do I Really Need to Go On?

Okay, enough is enough. And besides, I am sure that many of you have heard about the elephants and their stakes before, right?

But, I know that NONE of you ever heard it explained by using Maslow's Hierarchy of Needs.

My friends, stop worrying about the chains and stakes. They don't exist – except in your minds. Stop worrying about the other people in the herd. Put your energy into the thing that ONLY humans can do – DREAM!

CHAPTER 9
Deferred Gratification

Okay, if you have been an independent entrepreneur for any amount of time, you have doubtless come across the idea of deferred gratification. You know what it is. And, even if you had never heard of it before, the term "deferred gratification" is pretty much self-explanatory, right?

Let's take a look at the two words, and see just how simple the translation is:

1. Deferred – when we say something is "deferred," we mean it is put off for a later time. For example, you might hear that politicians "deferred a decision" until a later date. (Politicians are ALWAYS deferring decisions until a later date!)

2. Gratification – This is the reward you get from doing something. It could be something simple, like scratching an itch, or it could be something major, like paying off the final installment on your car loan. Gratification is a feeling of satisfaction.

So, when we refer to "deferred gratification" in a personal business sense, we are talking about things like "doing work now, so I can enjoy the rewards later."

An Example of Deferred Gratification

Do you remember when you were saving money to buy your first home? You needed a down payment – usually 20% of the purchase price. Let's say your first home cost $150,000. This means that you needed $30,000 down, and you would take a mortgage for the other $120,000.

When you first decided to buy a house, you had to take a really close look at your finances. For example, you were already paying rent on your current apartment. You also had a savings account. You also had other monthly expenses, and some kind of income. All of these things went into your planning for a home purchase.

Let's say, when you looked at your bank account, you only had about half ($15,000) of the down payment. It took you five years to save up that money. You don't want to wait an additional 5 years to save up the other half. What do you do?

There are only two choices if you want to save money up quickly. You either have to MAKE MORE money, or you have to CUT BACK on your expenses. These are your only two choices, and both of them require *deferred gratification*.

Choice 1 – Making more money. Most people work for someone else, so "making more money" isn't that easy. Maybe you can go to your boss and ask for a raise. But, how well did that go the last time you asked? You see, your BOSS doesn't want to defer HER/HIS gratification so you can buy a house. You can't say to your boss, "Why don't you make less money now, by giving me a raise. But, after I get that raise, I promise to work harder for you, and you will eventually get more money from my work." That won't work!

Or, you could take on another job, or start a business of your own. These choices will bring in more money, but they are going to require YOU to defer gratification. In either case, you are going to have to work harder right now, in order to get something you want later on. This is a classic form of deferred gratification.

Choice 2 – Cut expenses. – The second way to accumulate money quickly is to cut expenses. You can cut out things you are already doing – like dining out three or four times per week, or you can *refuse to buy* something that you really want NOW, in order to have more money for the things you want later. For example, let's say you have a car that is 5 years old, and has 70,000 miles on it. You are thinking, "I could certainly use a new car right now. This old car is starting to look a little worn out. I *deserve* a new ride! Besides, I need reliable transportation for my job." But, if you buy that car, you are going to have a car payment. This means you will not be able to afford a loan for the new home you want. So, in the end, you decide to drive the car for 4 more years, and be able to save up your down payment more quickly for the new home.

In either of the cases above – making more money, or cutting expenses – you are *deferring gratification*. In the case of making more money, you are working harder now, so you can enjoy the benefits later. In the case of cutting back on expenses, you are giving up the pleasure (gratification) of having a new car right now, so you can enjoy a much more meaningful gratification later on.

Deferred Gratification – no elephants need apply!

Remember our study of elephants in the last chapter? Elephants NEVER have deferred gratification. All the elephants do is sit around, chained to their stakes, *waiting* for someone to bring them food and water. When the trainers and handlers DO bring elephants water and food, no elephant thinks to himself, "Maybe I'll save some of this food for later. I remember yesterday, when I was so thirsty around 3 p.m., and I had to wait for dinner time to get more food and water. Today, I am going to set some aside."

NOTE: It does seem unusual that elephants do not remember that they were thirsty yesterday, because as the old saying goes, "An elephant never forgets!"

No Sleep-Walkers need apply

Now, human beings are smarter than the average elephant, right? So why do so many of us act like the elephants when it comes to deferring gratification? Why do so many people live paycheck to paycheck? They get money in (on payday) and they send it out (the first day after payday). They say things like, "I wish we could afford to buy a house, but we just can't seem to save up the down payment." The fact is, they will NEVER be able to save up the down payment, because they will always be spending all their money as soon as they get it.

No "Maslow's" need apply!

Now, let me give you something that probably NO ONE has given you before: an even deeper understanding of why *filling needs* is not as good as *building Dreams*.

If you are a follower of Maslow's Hierarchy, then you are always *back-filling* your most urgent needs. For example, if you suddenly realize you need a new car, you are going to buy it, because it fills a *need* for transportation. But, if you also feel a *need* for status, you are likely to buy a car that you really don't *need*, but it is a car that you *want*. (However, you are going to convince yourself you *need* that kind of car.) So, instead of saving for a house, you buy another car – and then take out a loan for it, with high payments. Now you don't have the down payment for the house, and you also can't qualify for a loan because your monthly payments are too high on the car (and all the other stuff you bought, but didn't pay cash for).

Remember, Maslow says that people will always try to fill their most pressing need. I agree with Maslow: MOST people do just that.

So, stop being Maslow-like, and start Dreaming and building for your future, and the things you REALLY want.

Dreams Are the Only Things Strong Enough To Defer Gratification

Folks, you have a choice. You can either stand there, thinking you are chained to a stake, waiting for someone to bring you a substandard level of rewards, or you can build your life, bit by bit, with a Dream in mind.

It won't be easy. You are going to have setbacks. You are going to experience *pain* along the way. You will wish you were just able to get everything you want, whenever you want it. It might even drive you a little crazy.

But, having a Dream, and deferring gratification so you can achieve something *spectacular* is worth it! People who have the discipline to *build* will have more of everything they want - Money, Love, Pride, Satisfaction – ANYTHING they want.

Here is the good news. If you learn how to defer gratification WISELY, in a process, you will only have to do the work for a short time. If you do it right, you can reduce the risk and the pain. If you follow a *process*, your life will be better, and it will be better faster!

CHAPTER 10

Minimizing Deferred Gratification – Filling the Pipeline

Here is the reason that most people are not willing to *defer their gratification*. They think in terms of LADDERS, instead of PIPELINES! This is a *Dream-killing*, vision-limiting, and energy-wasting view of life. It comes directly from the fact that the vast majority of people work for someone else – for forty or fifty years of their precious lives – and keep doing one task after another, day-after-day. It is a soul-sucking exercise that leaves you drained!

The Ladder

Here is how most people see their lives. They look ahead, and all they see is an endless ladder that they must climb. Sometimes, they might jump over a rung in the ladder, but then, they might get stuck on other rungs for years at a time. In order to succeed, or climb the ladder, they assume that they have to achieve one task (on a rung) before climbing up that rung to the next rung. Once there, they do all the work that is required on that rung, and then, maybe, they can climb one more rung. What are the rungs in your ladder? Well, if you are like the AVERAGE person, they might look like this:

Just Another Rung

A New Job

Your Promotion

Entry Level Job

Graduate School

School

<u>Rung 1 – School</u> – Everyone has to go to school, and that's a fact. In the United States, more and more of the population is going past high school these days. They might go to a technical school, but many more go to college. Once they are in college, they put off any thoughts of achieving anything of significance until they graduate. They assume, because people TELL them it is so, that they cannot achieve anything of significance until they have that degree. They are stuck on that rung for at least four years. Now, this is a shame, because young, college-age people have a lot to offer. In fact, is there any time in life when your energy is higher? This might be the time to learn some "out-of-school" lessons, as well as those great in-school lessons. For example, this is a great time to learn that you can do more than one thing at the same time. How about helping that college-age student look around, and explore some sort of hobby, interest, passion or dream that will propel them off that first rung while they are still in school? Isn't this a valuable lesson? It certainly is. And it can set them up for a lifetime of increased rewards.

By Waking Up while on the first rung, college students can make significant strides that will help them to live a better, more secure life.

Rung 2 – Graduate School – As a college professor, I see many young people today who are simply going through the motions, collecting a second degree – a Masters Degree. Look, I have no problem with more education. It can pay off great dividends in the long run. But, students should be careful to make sure that "getting a second degree" isn't just a way of postponing their Wake Up! The same strategies that apply to the first rung (a college education) also apply to any other rung that leads to a degree. Wake Up and start looking around.

College tuition is expensive. Student debt is out of control, at least in the United States. Those thousands of dollars you spent on a college education, and are now multiplying for a graduate degree, should be an investment, not just a debt. For example, while students are taking classes, they should also be using their time to build relationships, and learn what makes other people "tick," – not just in a classroom, but in the spaces they will occupy for the rest of their lives. This is valuable time, and it should be treated with the value it represents.

Best of all, the lessons you learn by working with others, and understanding their needs, will cost you NOTHING! There is no tuition, no extra charges. But, in the long run, your ability to help others, to work with them, and to build common, Wide Awake Dreams with them, will propel you off that second rung!

Rung 3 – The Entry Level Job – Did you ever hear someone say "Everyone starts off on the bottom rung and works their way up?" You see, you HAVE to start out on the bottom, because that is how everyone else did it. They will be mightily upset if they see you jumping over that bottom rung. So, they are going to create "on-the-job-training" systems where you SLOWLY learn to do your job.

Rung 4 – Your Promotion – Okay, after working for some years, you start to go up to the next rung. You get a raise. What do you do with that raise? You spend it on things you need, like a car and a house. But, do you pay CASH for those things? No, you get them on credit. Brother, you are going to be on this rung, or one just like it, for the rest of your life.

Rung 5 – A New Job – You learned (and earned) all that you are going to learn and earn on that job. Now, it is time to trade your vast experience, and all your education, for ANOTHER job, with another company. Why can't you just move up in the company where you are? Simple: they don't think you are really worthy of it. Think about it, they have been overworking you and under paying you for years. Why would they suddenly think you are worth more? You will never be worth more in this company. Better go somewhere else where they don't know you as well, so you can fool them into giving you more. Why is that position open in the new company? Well, the guy or gal who had it before you was stuck on that rung, and they went to some other company to get paid more. So, your new job is just something someone else didn't want anymore. Congratulations.

Rung 6 – Just Another Rung! – They all look pretty much the same. No reason to spend time in this book describing it.

When Rungs Turn Into a "JAR"

Take a look at the picture of the ladder again.

Do you see how rungs 6 – 12 are labeled "J.A.R.?" J.A.R. stands for "Just another Rung." And that's what *every* rung of your ladder is – *Just Another Rung*. You see, all the hard work you do, all the extra time you put in, all the saving and scrimping you do, and all the utter *nonsense* (insert your own word for it here) you put up with are moving you up to Just Another Rung. And, if you work a lifetime in this system, do you know where you will end up? You guessed it – *just another rung – a J.A.R.*

Folks, this is crazy, because you are better than that. You have a gifted mind. You are a good person. You took time out of your life to read this book. This isn't an easy book to read. It is a *challenging* book. It is asking you to re-consider all the "nonsense" you have lived with all your life. It is asking you to do something different. If you got this far in this book, you are an *extraordinary* human being. You shouldn't be on *Just Another Rung*. You should be living among the stars! You should be one of the very few people who breaks free of your elephant-holding bonds. (You know, the bonds that really don't exist at all!) You should be the kind of person who looks ahead, instead of being held back by every *need* that looms up and screams "scratch me, I am an itch."

You were born to be free. You were not born to endlessly climb a ladder, only to find yourself on *just another rung*.

Get off the ladder, and build a *pipeline*, and with continued work and effort, you should see some satisfaction and yes… self-actualization coming out of that pipeline.

The Pipeline

A number of years ago, one of my good friends, Burke Hedges, wrote a book called "The Parable of the Pipeline." It has been a long time since I read this book, but the basic story is this:

A small village had a well nearby. Every day, people in the village would fill up buckets from the well, and carry the water to their homes. One day, a man from the village built a pipeline from the well to the village. Instead of spending hours just carrying water, the villagers were able to put that time into more productive tasks. They all made more money, and the man who built the pipeline was paid to maintain it.

Well... I *think* that was the story. If it isn't, my apologies to Burke! But, even if it isn't exactly the story from the book, it is a darn good example of what "building a pipeline" is all about.

The Pipeline: Maslow vs. Dream Building

Now, I am going to talk more about the process of building a pipeline later in this book, because it is one of the things that Wide Awake people should do. But, for right now, I am going to help you make that difficult transition from sleep-walking (which we all do until we know better) to deliberate, Wide Awake activities that can help you reach your Dreams. Believe me, this is important, and I want to give you another tool to use when you work with other people, to help them reach their Dreams.

Let's take a look at the people in the village. They had a *need* for water. Maybe they needed it to drink, but they might also have needed it to water crops, wash clothes, water their animals, etc. How did they fill this need? They did it the same way that people in that village did it for centuries. They picked up buckets. Walked to the well. Filled those buckets, and then carried them all the way back to the village – or to wherever the water was needed.

Can you imagine that? Think about it. Did they EVER get a day off from carrying water? No! You see, water filled a basic need. We all need water to survive. If you have to carry water, you have to do it every day, forever!

Everyone in that village was sleep-walking their way through life. They were using the tools of the past to solve their problems of the present. Now, maybe this village was isolated, and so nobody had ever been anywhere else, and no one had ever seen or heard of a pipeline? Maybe that's why they never thought of doing it differently. But, the

NEED for water was so pressing that they never dared deviate from filling it every day.

Like Maslow said, they were motivated by their lowest, most pressing need.

But, one man had a Dream. He dreamt of a day when the water would come to HIM! How did he get that Dream? Well, maybe he traveled to another village, maybe a larger village, where they had a pipeline. Maybe he saw that pipeline and said, "Hey, this would change everything."

But, I can tell you this. If he did travel to another village, and saw their pipeline, and made the "a-ha" observation, he wasn't sleep-walking. He was Wide Awake! You see, he was looking forward, not backward. He wasn't thinking, "I better get home as soon as possible, because I have to carry water." He was thinking, "What could we do with our time if we didn't have to carry water all day, every day?" In fact, in his Wide Awake state of mind, he was probably saying, "Wow, look at that! These people have it all figured out. Wait, look at how big their village is. Look at how clean all their clothes are. Look at how *satisfied* everyone looks."

And then, he got a Dream. He started imagining just how prosperous he and his friends would all be when they could free themselves from the drudgery of carrying water. I have it on good authority that the first thing they did was build the pipeline, and the next thing they did was create an award-winning baseball team to entertain the people in the town, and to raise the prestige of their town. I have also heard that this man became a real estate agent, and sold properties that were farther from town, because these lands were suddenly habitable. (O.K., maybe that part is not true – but it certainly would be possible!)

Talk about a Win-Win Situation

Can you see what a difference you can make if you Wake Up? Wide Awake people see opportunities. Sleep-Walkers carry buckets of water. Your choice.

A Real-Life Example – *You will love this story!*

Now look. I am about to tell you a true story. This story is so amazing, that you are going to say, "That can't be how it happened." But, I am telling you it did happen this way, and I know for sure because the man in this story was a classmate of mine from college, and is, to this day, one of my very best friends in the world.

My friend was an engineering major in college. He is really, really smart. When he graduated, he went on to a well-known business school for an MBA. He combined his Engineering background, with his financial education, and became well-known for helping states and municipalities develop toll roads and turnpikes. He showed them how to estimate costs for building the roads (from his engineering background) and then how to pay for the roads with toll booths and other financial arrangements, such as Municipal Bonds (from his MBA knowledge).

Now, so far, you are probably saying, "Bill, what does this have to do with Pipelines, being Wide Awake, and Dream-building?" Well, hang on to your hats, because you are about to be amazed!

If you live in the United States, or Canada, you have heard about *EZ Pass*. If you live in another country, you probably have something similar. With EZ Pass, you get a transponder for your car, and then, when you go through a toll booth, you don't have to stop and hunt for the correct change. You simply drive through, and the EZ Pass equipment charges your credit card for the correct amount of the toll. Everyone has seen this system today, right?

Well, not so long ago, EZ Pass did not exist, but toll roads did. It was a real pain in the neck. You would be driving down the highway, and suddenly, all the traffic would slow down as people drove through the toll booths, realized they did not have the right change, and then had to search throughout the car, while they held you up in traffic! It was also expensive for the states and municipalities, because they had to hire all those toll takers!

But, my friend solved the problem one day, when he was watching a herd of dairy cows walk into a barn...

What!!!???? How Did *Dairy Cows* Solve the Problem?

You see, my friend was on some kind of project, and he happened to be on a large, very modern dairy farm, when the cows were coming back from the pasture. He noticed that the cows all had a sort of transponder embedded in their ears. My friend asked the farmer what the transponders do. The farmer explained:

"Those things help us keep track of the cows. We know if they are all back in the barn because those transponders keep track of them. In addition, those transponders measure how much feed they eat every day, and how much milk they produce. It has been an amazing system for us to use. It makes our lives so much easier."

Do you see the connection yet? Well, you probably do, because I laid it out for you (just like my friend did for me when he told me about it). But can you imagine just how *Wide Awake* my friend was when he put 2 + 2 together and came up with *EZ Pass*! Man, that guy was WIDE AWAKE!

But you see, he had a Dream. He wanted to make life easier for his clients (states and municipalities), and he wanted to be rich! He was *looking* for new opportunities. He could see that a business (taking tolls and paying for roads) was taking up entirely too much time, and costing too much. So, do you know what he did? He built a *pipeline*. He also built a HUGE company, and later sold it.

Have You Seen The Movie?

In the classic Christmas movie "It's a Wonderful Life", Jimmy Stewart plays George Bailey. In the movie, his daughter Zuzu hears a bell ring, and says "Teacher says, every time a bell rings an angel gets his wings."

Well, here is a new saying, "Every time a toll booth bell rings, Bill Quain's good friend makes about one-thousandth of a penny."

But guess what – those little bits of money really add up! Today, my friend is one of the very few *self-actualized* people I know. He has three beautiful homes (I know of three, maybe there are more). He is an author, who donated the proceeds of his book to his alma mater. He teaches at two, *really prestigious* universities – not because he needs the money, but because he really loves to share knowledge with students, and to help them succeed in life. He is a leader in his church. He, and his wife, are the two most generous people I ever met. They are really fantastic people.

What makes them so unique? What makes them so amazing? The answer is that they are traveling through this world with their eyes wide open. They are Wide Awake, always looking for interesting and rewarding things to do.

Will You Invent The EZ Pass?

Okay, you might be reading the story about my friend who *really* did invent the EZ Pass, and thinking, "Well Bill, do you expect ME to do something so BIG? I don't have that kind of education. I can't spend my life looking for the one big invention that will set me free. I can't take that kind of risk. What are you expecting me to do?"

Don't worry, this book isn't about doing HUGE, UNEXPECTED and INNOVATIVE things. It is really pretty simple. This book is just about Waking Up!

Think about it: I told you three stories so far in this book.

1. July 7, 1993, at 2:30 in the afternoon. My alarm clock went off.

2. Elephants aren't held in place by REAL tethers and stakes. They are held in place because they think *their* tethers and stakes are enough to hold them. People are the same way.

3. When everyone else is thinking about doing the same thing, day after day, for their entire lives, look for the pipeline that will set them free, and make you wealthy.

Yes, my friend was an exceptional inventor, but let's face it, the guy who built the pipeline for his village really didn't have to be that smart. I can tell you that I am not that smart! I couldn't have figured out how to develop EZ Pass, even if I had made the cow-to-turnpike connection.

What about you? Has your alarm gone off? Are you held by invisible (make that *non-existent*) bonds? Are you sleep-walking, or are you Wide Awake?

Folks, here is all you have to do to make HUGE changes in your life:

1. Get a big, motivating Dream.

2. Wake Up and Stay Awake.

3. Take your first steps towards freedom by picking up your feet and realizing that NOTHING is holding you back.

4. Find people who are looking back, filling their most pressing needs, and then find a pipeline that makes their lives better.

5. And, most importantly, to save yourself time and trouble, find other people who are already doing this, and JOIN THEM!

I have seen really ordinary men and women make remarkable changes in their lives, simply because they listened to their alarm clocks, woke up and stayed awake, and then found an opportunity to create a pipeline. And, the most successful of these people followed the examples of other successful people.

I tell you folks, this gets me so excited. I can't wait to tell you more.

CHAPTER 11
How to Fill a Pipeline

Remember this rule: You can't fill a pipeline from a bucket. Got it?

Take a look at the picture below. Someone is trying to fill a pipeline from a bucket. What is happening? All of the water is spilling out, over the opening of the pipeline. Even if you get SOME of the water into the pipeline, you are wasting too much water *and time*, because you now have to go fill up the bucket, and spend time trying to pour it into the pipeline. It just doesn't work.

Now, here is a rule to remember: Use a *funnel* to fill the pipeline. Got it? Take a look at the picture below.

A Funnel is Your Tool for Reaching a Dream

Do you remember the story about the man who built a pipeline to bring water to his village? Did you wonder how he did it? First, he built the pipeline. And then, he found a way to fill it. After that, he thought, "I wonder if there are more ways to fill this pipeline, and he built additional ways to fill it. He made a discovery – the most efficient pipeline is one that is easy to fill.

Here is what he did. His first thought about filling the pipeline was to put a funnel on the end closest to the well, and then teach people to pull buckets up from the well, and dump the buckets into the funnel. This worked fine, but he wanted to fill up the pipeline even faster, and have it carry more water.

He also thought to himself, "Right now, only one person can pour water into the pipeline at a time. I need to come up with a way to make this all a lot easier."

The Funnel Is the Key

Look, a pipeline is usually the same diameter, from the opening at one end, to the opening at the other. I mean, a "pipeline" usually means that you have one pipe, and for the most part, that pipe is the same diameter.

This makes it difficult to get things into the pipeline. Think of the pipeline in the village. It ran from the well (where the water was), to the other end, where people could use the water. When the villagers built the pipeline, they didn't build a HUGE, WIDE pipeline. That would have been too much work, and too expensive. They didn't need that big pipeline for their water. But, that small-diameter pipeline made it difficult to fill.

All it took was a simple *funnel* at the opening of the pipeline. The funnel was inexpensive to build. And, it allowed more than one person to fill that pipeline. In fact, for a very small investment, the villagers built a VERY BIG funnel, and when they needed a LOT of water (maybe in the morning when everyone was waking up, washing, and making breakfast), they could put a few more people on the funnel end, and the water really came gushing out the other end.

Big Dreams Need a Big Funnel, Not a Wide Pipeline

Hey, are you Wide Awake right now? If so, I think you are going to get a kick out of this next part. I am about to show you how to fill a pipeline quickly, and how to fulfill your dreams, not by trying to cram everything you need into a small pipeline, but by using a wide funnel to make life easier.

Here is how most people try to create a pipeline of income. They get a job. That job is a relatively small pipeline. Sure, it does create an income flow. It does create wealth. But, if you only have a job, then you are trying to cram all your dreams into a VERY small opening. You can spend a lot of time doing it, and the end result is that you are out of time, and you might not have the money you need to fulfill your dreams.

If you are putting all your hopes and dreams into a "job" pipeline, no one can really help you. There just isn't enough room at the top of the pipeline for someone else to get involved. And, there isn't any way to pour water from other sources into your pipeline. No matter how hard you try, only a small amount goes into the pipeline.

But, With A Funnel...

But now, think about how much different life would be if the entry to the pipeline wasn't restricted to your puny efforts! Imagine if other people could pour water into your pipeline, or if you could have water coming from a number of sources at the same time.

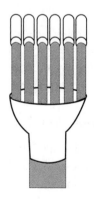

Okay, We Really Aren't Talking About WATER Here, Are We?

Look, you guessed it. The idea of water through the pipeline is just a metaphor. It is symbolic of your life. For most of us, we spend our entire lives thinking that we have just one pipeline for success. It is our jobs. At one end, we have a small opening, and we try to cram as much into that opening as possible. But, it is difficult, because the ONLY thing we have is our job.

On the other hand, we have a pipeline with a LARGE opening at the other end. It might not start out that way, but when you buy a home, buy 2 cars, buy food for the table, insurance, tuition, medical, etc. – well, that hole in the other end gets REALLY big! Pretty soon, you are faced with a situation that the resources you are able to cram into the pipeline are just a trickle when they drip out of that huge, "where did my money go?" end of the pipe.

And, sometimes the spending end of the pipe gets really, really wide – all of a sudden! Maybe it is a medical emergency. Maybe it is a wedding, a graduation, or something else. When that happens, even if you have a strong, steady flow out of the other end, your pipeline just isn't doing the job for you.

Fill the Funnels

How do ordinary men and women get more money (I mean water) into their pipeline? They build a big funnel on the front end, and then get the money (I mean water) from a number of sources. And, if they are really smart, they encourage others to add money (and I DON'T mean water!) into that funnel.

When You Suddenly Need More…

The good news about having a funnel, with multiple sources, is that you can quickly and painlessly add more input into your pipeline, as soon as you need it. You have the capability to add more, whenever you need it.

Funnels Are For Dreams, Pipelines Are For Needs

Let's go back to Maslow one more time. In his Hierarchy of Needs theory, you are always responding to the latest need. If you have a need at the lower level, you are not thinking about dreams. Instead, you are stuck at that lower level. If your pipeline does not have a funnel (a way to increase the capacity), you will NEVER get past the lower levels of the Hierarchy. You can't go higher, because the capacity of your pipeline is limited by what you can put into it, and what you can put into it is limited by the number of ways you can *fill* that pipeline.

However, suppose you are going beyond Maslow. You are waking up. In fact, you are WIDE awake! You have a huge dream – one that transcends the basic needs that most people spend their whole lives trying to fulfill. You want more. You are determined to HAVE more.

So, fit a funnel into the top of your pipeline, and start looking for other ways to fill that pipeline.

What Can You Fill A Funnel With?

It depends on what you want. For most people, finding alternative ways to get *money* into your pipeline is a good thing – even if you are still stuck in the Maslow Hierarchy. Money can *really* help to change lives. So, find alternative ways to get money into your pipeline.

I heard a great term just the other day, for new ways to get money into the pipeline. Some of the students in my class called it a "side gig." It is something *in addition* to your job. It is something that pours more money into your pipeline, just when you need it. To get multiple streams of income into your funnel, you need a funnel, because you just wouldn't have the time to cram more in without it.

A "side gig" is the current term for something other than your job. Hey, it works!

But, let's face it. Your dreams aren't just about *money*, are they? You also want a lifestyle – money *and* the time to spend it. So, you need to find a funnel that gives you both money and time.

Finally, you want a funnel that gives you a way to profit from the work of others. (Think of that picture above, where there is more than one person pouring water into the pipeline.)

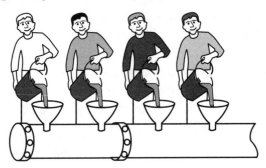

When you have big dreams, you will learn to look for FUNNELS that attract more people to your pipeline.

Want To Know More?

If you want to know more about how to build a pipeline, and adding a funnel, do what the guy who brought the pipeline to his village did:

1. Wake Up

2. Look for what OTHER people did

3. Duplicate their work, their ideas

4. Create an even bigger funnel by showing others how to do the same thing

And most importantly for right now...

Finish Reading This Book!

CHAPTER 12

The Best Way to Build a Dream – Wide Awake & S.M.A.R.T.

D o I need to say that date again? July 7, 1993, at 2:30 in the afternoon! That's when it happened – we woke up.

But, what happened after that date? How did we go about building intense, motivating, forward-looking Dreams that drove us to succeed? That is the subject of this chapter, and it is where the real work of Dream-building begins. By the end of this chapter, you will have a blueprint for designing your Dreams, and therefore, a blueprint for your Destiny.

Don't Start Day Dreaming Again

I have worked with many people, helping them build their Dreams into a framework for success. It isn't easy. It requires a lot of conversation and concentration. The biggest problem – the #1 BIGGEST problem is that many people either go back to sleep completely, or go halfway back to sleep, and begin Day Dreaming about their Dreams.

Folks, we have already discussed the difference between being Wide Awake, focusing on productive activities and actions, and being in a sleep-walking state, just Day Dreaming. Day Dreams are NOT productive. Day Dreams are not based in reality. They are dangerous, because you might *think* that you are Dream building, but you are really just postponing your success by postponing your acceptance of reality.

I never heard of anyone who produced anything from a Day Dream. Do you remember our discussions about how thinking about winning the lottery is just Day Dreaming? In a Day Dream, you imagine success, but never successful actions! For example, nobody ever Day Dreams about working really hard to achieve something worthwhile. Instead, we all Day Dream about *being* successful – never the steps it will take to *become* successful.

So, if you want to create believable, motivating and powerful Dreams that you can actually achieve, you have to be Wide Awake.

What Too Many People Do

Before I tell you how Jeanne and I went about setting up our Dreams, let me tell you what just too many people do. Like everyone else in the world today, I have been in plenty of meetings where someone says, "In order to be successful, you have to have a Dream. I want someone here to tell me what their Dream is." Without fail, someone says, "I want to be rich."

I have to admit, in the early days, when I was first learning that it was possible to create a different life than the one I presently had, I would have thought, "Good for you." It made sense.

Think about it. What is the FIRST thing someone says when they are asked what they want in life? For about 99% of the people I ever heard answer that question, the answer was a *very quick* "I want to be rich." That's not surprising. In the United States, where most states have two or three lottery drawings per week, MILLIONS of people buy lottery tickets – for one reason alone – to become rich. They see those lottery tickets as (quite literally) their ticket out of trouble, anxiety and stress. After all, if you have money, what is there to worry about?

Of course, not everyone said, "I want to be rich." A few people would say things like, "I want to help others." And, while this Dream might seem like it is better than, "I want to be rich," it is still not a good Dream. It is not motivating, it is not specific, and it is, frankly, pretty useless.

You see folks, you aren't creating a Dream because you think it is the right thing to do. You are creating a Dream so that when things get tough, you can *cling* to that Dream, and do the tough things necessary to attain it. If you just shoot off some trite saying, like "I want to be rich," or "I want to help people," that Dream is going to look pretty small, and maybe even invisible, the first time a tough challenge stands in your way. Anyone can say, "I want to be rich," even when they are half-asleep. Only the *brave* people will create Dreams that are truly challenging and motivating.

Any Excuse Will Do

So, what happens if someone you know tells you, "I want to be rich," and you say, "When?" The answer will be something like, "someday, maybe someday soon." But, if the person was being totally honest, the answer should be, "If I ever win the lottery, but besides that, *never!*"

And, if someday, you say to your friend, "Didn't you say you wanted to be rich? What ever happened to that?" What do you think your friend would say?

I'll bet it will be something like, "Well, you know that business I was getting into? It turned out…" Or, "I was all set to do something, but then my wife got sick…" or something along those lines.

Now sure, it is possible that the business this person was looking at turned out to be a dud. And, it is also quite possible that his wife did get sick, and he had to reset his priorities, but those things have NOTHING to do with his Dream! The fact that he "wanted to be rich" was thrown out the window, *the minute some obstacle presented itself*, is an indication (no, positive proof) that it wasn't a Wide Awake Dream. It was just a Day Dream.

Over the years, I heard thousands of different excuses. Some of them were very compelling. And, in some cases, the circumstances really did prevent the person from pursuing his/her Dreams. But in the end, an excuse is an excuse – no matter how compelling. And, a Day Dream is just a Day Dream – and is NEVER compelling!

What Jeanne and I Did

Later in this chapter, we will discuss the *reasons* you need to build a strong Dream, but first, let me tell you what Jeanne and I did when we heard our alarm going off, on July 7, 1993.

On July 8th, we loaded our car and headed back to our home in Orlando. It was a three hour drive. Along the way, while we were still in the car, we began the first of many discussions about *exactly* what we wanted in life. We had just seen those people on the back of the yacht, laughing and having a good time. Our first thought was, "We would like to live like that." After all, laughing on the stern deck of a huge yacht looks like a lot of fun, right? But, that was just a Day Dream! It was not our real, Wide Awake, Motivational Dream. It was a great place to start, but it was no place to finish.

A Little Dose of Reality

At that time, Jeanne and I had a pretty great lifestyle already. I was a college professor, with some businesses on the side. Jeanne was a full-time, stay-at-home Mom. She spent 19 years working with me on our side businesses, and raising the kids full time. On July 8,1993, she was four months pregnant with our younger daughter. As we talked about our Dreams, on that car ride back to Orlando, we always came back to our first priority – keep Jeanne at home with the kids.

For us, Dream-building always had two parts to it. We were very specific about what we wanted in life. AND, we were realistic in determining what that would take! For example, when Jeanne decided to be a stay-at-home Mom, we knew we still wanted to live well. One of our first decisions was that we would have to create multiple streams of income, because our lifestyle was not going to be possible with just my university pay. And, while the decisions we made were scary at first, working together to build both our dreams and our income, was very exciting. It was *habit-forming*, because once we started, we just didn't want to stop.

So, when we started building our Dreams, Jeanne and I looked at *categories* of our life, and *prioritizing* what we wanted to be able to do, and how we wanted to be able to live – and then we set about creating *income streams* that would allow us to live our Dreams.

We Never Said...

We never said, "I want to be rich," or, "we want to help others." That just wasn't in our vocabulary. We both knew that neither of those statements would last longer than the first time we had a challenge. Instead, we began with statements about the way we wanted to live. Here are a few examples:

1. We want to have a home on the water, where we can fish, go boating, and enjoy the natural beauty of the water.

2. We want a home with at least four bedrooms, and two bathrooms. The house should be big enough so that we can have guests visit us.

3. We want to take at least two big vacations each year. One of them will be to Ocean City, New Jersey. I was raised in Ocean City, New Jersey, and I used to own a home there. We went there every summer for two weeks, and rented a vacation home. All of my sisters and my brother rented homes there, and all of the cousins, including our daughters, would spend time together each summer in Ocean City.

4. We wanted to be able to pay for our children's education.

5. We wanted to specifically be able to help our parents as they were getting older. This included regular visits to see them, flying them down to Florida to spend time with our family, and the ability to help them financially. One set of parents needed that help eventually, and we were able to give it to them.

These were just some of the goals/Dreams that we developed, and they came from S.M.I.L.E. statements. It was a wonderful exercise for Jeanne and me, as we both shared these Dreams.

We Didn't Go Crazy!

I was in a Business Opportunity meeting once, and the presenter was a very successful business leader. He was talking about Dream building. He asked a young man in the front row a simple question: "How much would you need to make per year in this business in order to be satisfied?" The young man answered, "$100,000." The young man was serious.

The presenter and I were speaking in private after the meeting, and he had some interesting observations about the young man's answer. The presenter said, "That guy has never made $100,000/year in his life. In fact, I would be surprised if he ever made $50,000. But, he isn't going to accept my business opportunity unless he can make $100,000! Isn't that just crazy!"

Folks, here is a great example of how someone used a *Day Dream* as an excuse. This young man was challenging the presenter to show him how he could make $100,000/year. This is just nuts! It is completely unrealistic to think that anyone can make a "yes" or "no" decision on a business – if their *bottom line limit* is more than double the amount of money they are making each year, from a job that they spend 40 – 50 hours/week, every week of the year!

Let's say that young man was making $40,000/year. (I know it wasn't that much, because this was twenty years ago, at least! It was probably more like $25,000, but the exact amount really isn't relevant here.) If that young man was being paid $40,000/year, it was because he was doing work that his employer valued at $40,000/year. How could this guy think he would suddenly go from $40K to $100K? His work would have to be so much more valuable than it was that day.

Think about this. If you are making $40,000/year, wouldn't it be worth some effort to make an additional $10,000 in a side business? That's 25% more than he was making now. Wouldn't that make a difference? Of course it would.

Now, let's take it a little farther. What kind of life was he leading at $40,000? (Remember, this was years ago.) This young man probably had a nice apartment or small home. He had a wife and at least one child. His wife was working. They probably took a vacation each year. They probably each had a car. If he had an extra $10,000/year – *every year* – would he be living better? Of course he would.

Now, let's say he wanted a really nice home, and wanted to be able to buy a new, fancy truck. Would that $10,000/year extra cover that? No. But, if he made some serious changes in his life, and spent some time building a business, he might be able to afford to have the big house and the big truck!

The point is this: You want to build Dreams that are realistic for you. If you suddenly yell out to the world that you "will be rich," or that you "will make $100,000/year," you are setting yourself up for failure. And, you are setting yourself up to let almost *any* excuse substitute for your Dreams.

You see, *reality* is very important in successful Dream-building. You need to be wide-awake, and you need to have some perspective. This young man was NOT realistic. He had no perspective. To him, creating a dream was simply a matter of wishful thinking. In his mind, all you had to do to have a Dream was to shout it out at a meeting. Instead of taking the opportunity seriously, he was showing off, and challenging the speaker. Instead, he should have quietly looked at his circumstances, and *challenged himself!* This young man cheated his family out of an opportunity to have a better life.

On The Other Hand, Jeanne and I were Already Doing Well on July 7, 1993

By 1993, Jeanne and I had already established several income streams. I had my job as a professor, PLUS my businesses. We knew how to make money. So, we were able to establish some pretty big Dreams, like "a four-bedroom/2bath house on the water, with a boat in the backyard." We had the *vehicles* that could carry us to our goals, and we were already associating with people who had that kind of lifestyle.

But, look at what our first Dream was – "To let Jeanne stay home with the kids, while they were growing up." And, we had accomplished that Dream. We were living that Dream. So, when we had our Wake-Up call on July 7, 1993, we were ready to build even BIGGER Dreams.

Remember, You Are Not Day Dreaming About The Lottery

Friends, I don't know where you are in life right now. You might be young or old, money-rich or money-poor, time-rich or time-poor. You might have a family. Maybe you have a great profession, where things are going well financially, and you are dreaming about having the *time to spend that money*. I just don't know you – *personally*. But, I know you as a human being. And, like most human beings, we want it all, and we want it right now. That's why the lottery is so appealing.

But, this is a book about being wide awake, and building strong, lasting and *realistic* dreams. You can have it all… you really can. But, you can't have it all tomorrow. I am showing you how to *build* a dream, and *build* a lifestyle. Building something always takes time. However, if you spend the time building a strong foundation, you will have a strong, dependable and wonderful lifestyle – *that lasts a lifetime!*

S.M.A.R.T. Dreams are SMART Business

What is a S.M.A.R.T. Dream? S.M.A.R.T. stands for:

S. – Specific – A *specific* Dream is easy to identify. It has nothing to do with generalizations, like, "I want to be rich." For our "Dream House," we were VERY SPECIFIC – "On the water, with our boat in the backyard, four bedrooms/two baths."

M. – Measurable – Again, we could measure our "Dream house" Dream. We searched the market, and discovered exactly how much it would cost us. We were always looking at real estate in the areas that interested us. (We still do this today! In fact, we are flying down to Florida next week to look at investment property. We keep up with property prices in the areas where we like to invest, and the area where we live.)

A. – Achievable – We knew we could do this! How did we know? We knew the numbers – the cost of homes on the water, and the amount we had coming in from businesses and my job. We knew it would take some time, and LOTS of effort, but we also knew we could do it.

R. – Realistic – We weren't looking at getting 5.2 waterfront acres with a 10,000 square foot house. Our goals were definitely realistic!

T. – Timely – We set a time limit for our Dream "live on the water." We wanted to do it in 5 years. Well… it took us all 5 of those years, but we did it! The time limit helped us defer some gratification, and it motivated me to take on more projects and work in my businesses (while making sure I always did a GREAT job on my job. I wanted to protect my source of income).

S.M.A.R.T. Dreams Keep you Awake on Your Journey

Unlike winning the lottery, building S.M.A.R.T. Dreams, and *achieving*, them is a journey. It isn't a one-time event. It took Jeanne and me 5 years to move from our home in Orlando to our home (on the water) in Miami Beach. And, even after we arrived on the water, our journey was not over. Our first boat in Miami Beach was a 22-foot sailboat. That was great for a while, but we soon realized we wanted something bigger and faster in order to go deep-sea fishing. We bought and sold several boats, before finally buying the "HurriQuain," a 30-fishing/cruising boat. (Don't you love the name "HurriQuain) We didn't just go from "no boat" to "Dream Boat." *We built our Dreams, and then built our ability to meet those Dreams.* Life is a journey. When you recognize this, you are well on your way, growing from Day Dreaming, to Wide Awake, Motivational Dreaming.

S.M.A.R.T. Dreams Give You X-Ray Vision

IMPORTANT: the purpose of a Dream is twofold. First, it is the goal you want to attain. Second, it is the only thing that will give you X-Ray Vision. X-Ray Vision allows you to see through obstacles and challenges, and clearly visualize the rewards that are ALWAYS hidden behind those obstacles and challenges.

Let's take an example of a typical couple that wants to make some big changes in their lives. This couple is in their early 40's, with two kids in high school. Let's say that couple has a Dream – and that Dream is to retire early from their jobs, and move to a beach area. Their Dream may look something like this:

We want to retire from our current jobs by the time we are each 55, which is 12 years from now. After retirement, Mike (the husband) would like to work in a job that is low pressure, and that will give him the winter months off. Julie (the wife) would like to do the same thing. In the wintertime, the couple would like to be able to play golf, and travel to see grandchildren (fingers crossed!). The couple is willing to sell their current home, but they would like to pay off the remaining $150,000 on their mortgage, so they can use the proceeds from the house to pay off their beach house, and live life without a mortgage. Their ideal lifestyle would be to have lots of friends, be able to visit and help their children, live debt free, and have time to travel.

The couple has done research, and they know exactly how much it will cost to buy a desirable beach house. They estimate that they can each make about $25,000 per year at "no-hassle beach jobs." They estimate they will need an additional $100,000/year to give them the income they need to live the life they want, for a total of $150,000. (This might not sound like enough money, but remember, this couple will be living debt-free, and they have a sizable amount in their 401K accounts. In addition, they have 12 more years to add to that total.) They want to find ways to create more income NOW, so they can continue to save, pay off debt, and start building an income stream that they can use to achieve their goals.

This is a very nice Dream. Let's see how S.M.A.R.T. it is.

Specific – This couple has the location of their dream home picked out, and they know how much beach houses cost there. They have been looking at real estate, and they know how much their current house is worth. They both have specific ideas about the kinds of jobs they would take at the beach, and how they would spend their free time in the winter.

Measurable – This couple knows the numbers! They have a target income for their semi-retirement ($100,000) and they are giving themselves 12 years to build their side income to that level. Is this Dream measurable? Absolutely. They will know exactly when they have achieved it, just from the numbers.

Achievable – Is this Dream achievable? I don't know this couple, but a lot of it looks reasonable. For example, they have already compared the value of their current home to the prices of beach homes. Currently, they have a $150,000 mortgage, and they are giving themselves 12 years to pay it off. That is a little more than $10,000/year in order to pay it off. I think that is do-able. Will they have enough money to live their lifestyle? That is a good question, but one I can't answer. On the other hand, it certainly seems reasonable that they could increase their beach income if needed.

Realistic – Well, people do retire at 55 – especially if they are really "semi-retiring". It seems to me that this couple isn't talking about stopping work altogether, they ARE talking about a lifestyle change. That certainly seems realistic.

Timely – No question about it, this couple has put timelines on this Dream.

Challenges and X-Rays

The couple shares their plans with some family members. Chuck (Mike's brother) *immediately* jumps in with a story about his friend who retired at 55, and then, he missed the excitement of working. "This guy was a real go-getter, just like you Mike. The first day he retired, he was sure he had made a mistake. I think you are crazy to want to move to the beach. It is lonely down there in the wintertime. And besides, people like us never retire early."

Mike didn't even need X-Ray glasses to look through this observation. Mike knows that his brother has never really had much ambition. Mike realizes that Chuck is afraid of losing his close friendship with Mike. But, Mike also realizes that he isn't living his life for his brother – or for anyone else.

Two years later (and two years into their timeline for retiring), Mike is offered a big promotion at work. However, it means he will have to work a lot more hours, and do a lot more traveling. This means it will be more difficult for Mike and Julie to build a side income. Mike wants the ongoing income of a side business more than he wants the raise. His X-Ray vision allows him to look right through this promotion, and see that it will not help him reach his Dream.

Julie gets laid off from her great job. This puts a real dent into their Dreams, because they were depending on her income to help pay off that mortgage. But, Mike and Julie gave themselves a cushion. They wanted to be semi-retired at 55. With this new development, they might have to push that to 58. While Julie is looking for a new job, she puts more time into the side business. Julie uses her X-Ray vision to see the dangers of depending on someone else to hire her. She saw firsthand just how easy it is for a boss to lay her off. Julie and Mike are more eager than ever to build a new stream of income, because they don't want the stress that comes from depending on a job – which can go away at any time.

Your Dream Is Your Beacon

Folks, just like Mike and Julie, Jeanne and I kept our Dreams in front of us at all times. If something happened, or if someone tried to reduce our income or potential for enjoying life, we simply kept our focus on the Dream, and found ways to work around our obstacles. It wasn't important to us, unless it helped us reach our Dreams.

A Personal Note

Many of my readers know this already, but for those of you who do not, I would like to tell you that I am almost completely blind. I walk with a white cane, cannot drive a car (which is great news for anyone on the street!), and I can't read print, or see faces. My abilities are very limited by my handicap. It makes things pretty tough, I can tell you that.

Imagine what you would do if you lost your eyesight. How would it change your ability to make money, build relationships, and stay fit and healthy? There is probably no way for you to imagine just how difficult life could be when you lose one of your senses.

I am lucky, however, because I *knew* I was losing my eyesight. Each year, it gets worse. But, each year, I get better at dealing with it, and each year, I learn new ways to make money and thrive. I am in a race with time, because at this point, I have so little eyesight left that losing more (which is going to happen) will be devastating. One of the reasons that I am setting up ongoing streams of income based on hard work and effort, is because right now, I am still able to do it. In another couple of years, who knows?

But guess what, YOU have something going on as well. You probably aren't losing the rest of your eyesight, like I am. But, guess what? SOMETHING is going to happen to you. It might be a medical issue. It might be an unexpected layoff, or a divorce. Life is life! No matter what your Dreams and plans are, you can be certain that something bad can happen. For me, I am lucky (in a way.) I know that something bad is happening to me. I know that my time to work and make money is limited.

Okay, maybe nothing bad or unexpected will happen to you, but do you really want to take that chance? Don't procrastinate. Never put off your dreams. I am going to let you in on a little secret. Ready? Here it is:

Some people NEVER run into bad luck – like a health setback, or a layoff, or a divorce. But, procrastinating is habit-forming. It gets easier and easier to fool yourself into thinking you have plenty of time. Do you remember what we said about daydreaming? If you are putting things off, and saying to yourself, "There is no hurry. I have plenty of time..." then guess what? This is Daydreaming! It is walking around, half asleep.

Each year that you postpone your Dream-building, each year that YOU postpone your side income streams, YOU are in more danger.

I don't care how old you are, or how young you are. It is time to start. Get S.M.A.R.T. Wake Up! Build your Dreams, and then find a way – any way – to make them come true. And, never let anyone or anything turn you from your Dreams.

I know you can do it! I did, and have the additional challenges of being blind!

CHAPTER 13

Categorize and Prioritize –
Money, Sunny and Honey

I mentioned earlier in this book that Jeanne and I *categorized and prioritized* our Dreams. I would urge you to do the same thing. But, most people have a little trouble doing this, so let me show you a fantastic *system* that not only makes this relatively simple to do, it makes it really fun and interesting as well.

Checklist Analysis – Your Key to Categorizing and Prioritizing Your Dreams

The first thing you need to learn is a VERY simple technique called "Checklist Analysis." Now, this might sound a little complicated. But, stick with me, and I will show you how to do this in a snap!

What is checklist analysis? I think the best way to explain it is to think about the last time you were asked to fill out a comment card at a restaurant, store, etc. You know what a comment card is, right? It is simply a place where you write comments! (Duh!) Nowadays, we find comment cards online, not just on a physical card.

Have you ever left a review on *Yelp* or *Amazon*? These are digital comment cards. We look at them all the time, whenever we are trying to decide on which item to buy, or which restaurant to visit. For example, suppose you are traveling to a new city, and thinking about going out to dinner. The first thing you might do is to look at the customer reviews (digital comment cards) that former customers have written. Maybe you are trying to decide between two steak houses. One of them has 45 reviews, with an average rating of 4.8, and the other has only 13 reviews, and the ratings are split. The average is pretty good 4.1, but there are a lot of negative comments. If the prices are relatively the same, you are probably going to choose the restaurant with more ratings, and a high average score, right?

Well, this is checklist analysis. You didn't just look at the scores, you looked at the comments as well. In your mind, you broke the comments into categories, and you prioritized them. For example, let's say one person at the highly rated restaurant really criticized their wine list. They might have written the following comment, "I was seriously offended that they did not have a bottle of the Montrachet Nebulizer Haute Criminal from 1965. They only had the 1974, and that was a terrible vintage. What kind of steak house is this?"

But, let's say you don't drink wine, or at least, you don't drink THAT kind of wine. In your mind, you are going to put that comment into a category (wine) that isn't important to you, and give it a low priority when making a decision about that restaurant.

On the other hand, if the comments about the amount of food you get for the price are very good, and you like getting more while paying less, you might categorize that comment into a category called *Huge Portions*. You might give it importance when you use it to make a decision, as in "Honey, we need to go to THIS place, because I get 3½ pounds of meat for just $15!"

You see? You have been doing checklist analysis for years! I'll bet you are going to pick up this technique very quickly for categorizing and prioritizing your Dreams.

By The Way…

I must tell you that I made a LOT of money over my career by simply doing a checklist analysis for clients – primarily in the hotel and restaurant industries. Even before the internet made it possible to do Digital Comment Cards, I would help restaurants analyze their old-fashioned comment cards, and come up with plans of action to make improvements at the restaurant, based on the categories we identified. Let me give you a quick example from a restaurant, and then you will see how important checklist analysis is for categorizing and prioritizing.

Suppose a restaurant had those old-fashioned comment cards. They take the comments from the cards, and break them into a line-by-line set of comments. Here is what they found:

1. The room was so cold.

2. My server was very nice, but she didn't know what she was doing.

3. I kept feeling a draft on my back. I was uncomfortable.

4. My server kept bringing us food we didn't order.

5. The lady at the next table asked them to turn down the air conditioning, and then I was too hot.

6. I love this place, because I get free desserts when my server forgets to put them on the check.

Okay, let's just take these 6 comments. Do you see any patterns here? Is there any way to *categorize* these comments? I see two categories. The odd-numbered comments all seem to be about the temperature/comfort/air conditioning of the room. The even-numbered comments seem to be about training and server knowledge issues. If I was the manager in this restaurant, which category would I prioritize? Well, I don't know how to fix a cooling/heating system, and it does look like some people thought it was too cold, and at least one person commented that it was too hot, so I might prioritize the training/knowledge category. In fact, I know that category is costing me money, because I am giving away free desserts! The people who are too cold can put on sweaters!

Do you see how simple this can be, and how meaningful it can be when you are deciding where to put your focus and spend your time? For example, suppose you did a comment card list for your Dreams, and you saw one category that had FAR more comments than the others. And, suppose those comments set off your alarm clock? Wouldn't you prioritize actions that would build that Dream, or at least, your chances of success in that area?

Building S.M.A.R.T. Dreams From a Checklist

Now, I know you are not building your future on creating a restaurant, as you read *Wake Up & Dream*! So, I am going to give you an example of how to build S.M.A.R.T. Dreams from a checklist. In order to do this successfully, you should create a series of *Comment Cards* – based on your life right now. In other words, pretend you are a CUSTOMER in your present life. You are going to come up with comments that capture the good and bad in your life. Sound Crazy? It Should! It IS crazy. It is crazy because almost NO ONE you know is doing this. But, almost NO ONE you currently know is Wide Awake and building Dreams either, so if you think that is a good system, then you are acting even more crazy, because you are going back to sleep – *on the only life you are ever going to have.*

Later, I am going to give you some more tips and tricks for doing a comment checklist for your life, but for now, let's just take a look at an example – using just 6 comments (like the restaurant comments above).

Comment Card for YOUR life (an example)

1. We haven't taken a real vacation in a few years. We are always too busy to get away.

2. We both work full time, and yet we don't have enough money to pay the bills.

3. I hate spending so much time in traffic, when I commute every day. I get to work (or come home) so frustrated and angry.

4. We haven't even begun to save money for the kids' college tuitions, and the oldest child is in sophomore year of high school.

5. I have a chance for a promotion at work, but if I take it, I will be traveling even more than I am now.

6. I am feeling so tired all the time. It really affects my relationships with my family.

Okay, does this look like comments from YOUR life? If not, no worries, at least you can see what kinds of comments you MIGHT have from your life.

Now, look at the six comments above. Do you see any patterns? Are there any areas that come up again and again? Comments 1, 3 and 5 seem to be about *time issues*, right? But, %1 – no time for vacations – could also be a money issue, because, if you had the *money*, you might suddenly have the *time* to go on vacations, right? Certainly, #4 – saving money for the kids' college tuitions is a *money* issue. And, #6 – feeling so tired that it affects relationships – might, at first, seem like a *relationship* problem, but it might be a *time* problem as well. For example, if this person had more *time* to go to the gym, she/he might be in better health, less tired, and better able to balance work and family issues.

S.M.A.R.T. Dreams Solve Problems – and lead to better comments

In the restaurant example, the manager was able to use the comment checklist to identify problems, and prioritize actions. As you are about to learn, using life comment cards can help you do the same thing. For example, if you see that *money* is an issue, your S.M.A.R.T. dreams should focus on building a side income so that you can *stop the pain* caused by your lack of money. If you find time problems, your S.M.A.R.T. Dreams should focus your priority on changing things in your life so that you have more *time*. Of course, sometimes your time problems are really *money* problems! (Take a look at #1 again. Is it really a matter of *time* that is keeping you from your vacations? It might be, but then again...)

Throughout the rest of this book, we will be focusing on specific techniques and tactics that will help you use common sense, and your own observations, to pinpoint the kinds of challenges you now face, and how to solve those challenges by building S.M.A.R.T. Dreams – and acting on them

The 80/20 Rule and Dream Building Success

About a hundred years ago, an Italian Economist named Wilfredo Pareto noticed something about the wheat crops in his native country. He discovered that *80% of all the wheat produced in his country came from just 20% of the acreage.* Then, he started looking at other things, and found that the 80/20 rule applied to them as well. (That is why it is still called the "Pareto Principle" today.)

You know that the 80/20 rule really does work out, don't you? For example, if you look at your problems and challenges, you would notice that approximately 80% of your problems come from just *20% of the categories of those problems!* Okay, now maybe it isn't going to be exactly 80/20, but in most cases, there are definitely relationships, and you will find that a few things cause a majority of the problems.

Look at the people around you at work. Do all of them make equal contributions towards getting things done? Probably not. Isn't it true that a *few* of them get *most* of the work done? (And, of course, you are among the few!)

It is amazing how often we can find a few things that cause us the most trouble, or a few things that can give us the biggest rewards. Let's go back to your job. Are ALL the tasks you perform there important? Are there some that you can stop doing, and nobody would ever notice? Well, that happened to me once.

My Battle with Useless Reports

At one university where I taught, we had to fill out 12 reports each year. One year, I didn't fill out any reports. It wasn't long before my boss said, "Hey, where are those 5 reports?" What did I learn? Seven of the reports did not have to be done.

Now I am not suggesting you try this at work, and I am not saying that 5 out of 12 is anything close to the 80/20 split, but I am saying that the principle applies, and you should use it to build successful Dreams.

And, even more importantly, applying the Pareto Principle (the 80/20 rule) is a sign that you are Wide Awake, and that is always good for you.

CHAPTER 14

Building Your Dreams by Building a Checklist

Are you Wide Awake and ready to kick your Dream-Building into high gear? Okay, then this is what you should do next.

1. Work with a partner – If you are part of a couple, AND if both of you are prepared to work together, than you have a built-in partner. If you are not part of a couple, or if the other person is not working with you to build a Dream, find someone who will spend some time with you. You need someone to share this with.

2. Get ready to write down statements in a list. I prefer to use a spreadsheet, because it becomes easier to sort things out into categories later. However, you can also use index cards, and write down one statement on each card.

3. Write your "Dream" Statements. – What is a "Dream Statement?" Simple. All you have to do is to start writing down statements about the kind of life you want to have, the kind of things you will have in that life, and the things you want to have all around you.

   a. For example, you might write the statement: I want to have a 3 bedroom house, with a pool, in my current neighborhood. I want to have that house within 5 years.

     b. Or, you might write: My kids are going to college in ten years. I want to have $25,000 set aside for them by that time.

4. Take your time. You might need more than one session to write out all your Dream Statements.

5. After you have written all your Dream Statements, start going through them, looking for *Categories*. Make a list of the categories you discovered, and assign each category a number. For example, you might discover you have categories called "Education," "Where we live," "Travel," etc.

6. Next, separate the Dream statements into those categories.

     a. If you are using a spreadsheet, create an open column in column A, and write the number of the category that best fits this statement, into column A. When you have finished this task, simply "sort" the Dream Statements by telling the spreadsheet to "sort by Ascending number" in column A. This will rearrange all the Dream Statements into the Categories.

     b. If you are using index cards, sort the statements into piles, by category.

7. Take a look at the items in each category, and then decide where to prioritize your time. If one category seems more important than the others, make this your first priority, and get to work!

Simple? YES! Valuable? ABSOLUTELY!!

Folks, this is one of those simple tools that will truly change your life! I am not exaggerating when I tell you this. It WILL change your life.

Look at what you will have:

★★★Positive, motivating and powerful Dream Statements that will describe your life when you attain your Dreams. I mean it, these are BIG, BIG, BIG!

★★★Categories of Dream Statements – This might be the first time in your life that you ever organized your future this way. Believe me, just the process of creating *categories* can be a game changer. Get it on paper (or on your computer), and make it real.

★★★Priorities – You can't possibly do all these things at once. When you do your checklist analysis, you will be forced to *choose* where you want to put your energy first.

Checklist Bonus – Look for 80/20 Opportunities

Okay, are you ready to "kick this up a notch"? Apply the Pareto Principle to your prioritization. Look through the categories, and see if you can find similarities between some of the Dream Statements. Are there one or two things you can do that would help you reach MANY Dream Statements? For example, if you were to develop a side income, would it solve more than one problem? How much will you need? When do you need it?

This can be a powerful tool for motivating yourself, and others. One of the biggest complaints/excuses that people use is that they do not have time for any changes in their lives. But, what if you can find one or two things that will make *dozens* of things better? This is the Pareto Principle at work. And believe me, it really works!

Money, Sunny and Honey – the super categories

Jeanne and I have been doing this for years, and we know how powerful it is, and how well it works. But, we are always looking for ways to make it easier and faster. After working with all kinds of categories, we began to see a pattern. We found that 99% of all categories will fit into 3, SUPER CATEGORIES: Money, Sunny and Honey. Let's take a look at these Super Categories, and see how they will impact your life.

1. Money – Okay, this is pretty easy to figure out, isn't it? So many of the Dream Statements people write are centered on some kind of money issue. For example, take a look at the two statements we wrote just a page or two ago –

"3 bedroom house with pool, and set aside $25,000 for kids' college." In the end, aren't these both money issues? Even statements like "travel to Europe for a month" could be a money issue. (It might also be a *time* issue, but then, time is something you can afford – *if you have the money!*)

2. Sunny – Sunny is a word we use to describe things like your mental, physical and emotional health. For example, did you ever hear the expression, "She has a *sunny* disposition"? If you want your life to be Sunny, you need good health (mental, physical and emotional). For example, suppose one of your Dream statements was "I want to lose fifteen pounds and keep it off, so that I will feel better about myself." (Hey, losing weight, looking good and feeling good is a very worthwhile Dream Statement! In fact, we encourage people to get fit and healthy. It reduces stress, and make you happier.) Now, some people have chronic health issues. Believe me, I know a LOT about that – I am almost totally blind, and there is no cure for my problem. However, I can *maximize* my health in other ways. I will never see again, but I can keep in good shape by running and working out. How about you? Are you maximizing your "Sunny"? Don't forget to take care of your emotional and mental "Sunny" as well. Reduce stress by becoming the best "you" that you can be.

3. Honey – These are your relationships, as in "Honey, I'm home." Relationships are so important for both personal and business success. Look for positive, successful people, and create relationships with them. Build a relationship with one, special person. Building relationships will require you to grow and change. Take a look at your face in the mirror. Notice you have two ears, and only one mouth. Here is a hint for building relationships – listen twice as much as you talk!

Do I Have My Priorities Wrong?

When I talk about Money, Sunny and Honey in stage presentations, or even one-on-one, I am sometimes criticized because people say, "I think you have your priorities all wrong. You are putting Money first. Shouldn't you put Honey first? After all, people are more important than Money."

Well, I have this to say: "If there isn't any Money, it isn't going to be very Sunny, Honey!"

Don't let people make you feel bad because you have a strong desire to create wealth. Wealth is a fundamental necessity for a Healthy and Sunny life. Money is important for relationship building. If you have Money in your life, you are going to have more time for other people. If you have Money in your life, you have the ability to take trips, spend time with others, help other people, and do all the things that make you feel good about yourself.

Believe me, I am not saying that Money is the most important thing in life. But, I am saying that it is VERY important, and can free you up to enjoy your life, and the people in it.

More About Money

I have been writing about money, speaking about money, and teaching about money for most of my adult life. I will say the following about money:

1. I LOVE having money. You see, I tried NOT having money, and it was really, really terrible! I mean it, it was BAD! Don't believe me? Okay, try this experiment. Get rid of all your money, and start spending money on your credit card. In 30 days, you will clearly see the impact of NOT having money. When those credit card bills come in, and you cannot pay them, how does your Sunny look? How does your Honey feel about your behavior?

2. It is amazing how many people are still telling others, "Money isn't important." I mean it – it just drives me crazy!

Why are people so afraid to admit that money is important? And, if money isn't important to people, why are they buying lottery tickets, or even worse, going to a job they don't like, week after week, year after year?

3. It is relatively easy to make more money. BUT, it is relatively difficult to make more money the same way you have been making money for your entire adult life – on a job.

4. Most people make money by giving up time. So, if they want more money, they have to spend TIME to get it. Soon, they are running dangerously low on Time. When you run low on Time, you start suffering in the other two Super Categories – Sunny and Honey.

5. So, how is it easy to make more money if it can't be made on your current job? The answer is simple, but it takes some willingness to face reality. There are companies out there who want you to help them make more money, and they are willing to pay you to do it. When you find this opportunity, look for someone who has done this before and get advice from them, and try to duplicate them. A Mentor or coach-like person is a valuable asset, if you can find one.

6. Don't believe me? Go to Amazon.com. Find a product you like, and that you know other people will like. Create an account with Amazon, and start sending out emails and texts to people you know. When they click on your link, go directly to Amazon, and buy that product, you get paid by Amazon.

7. Want to make even MORE money? Find a company that does exactly what Amazon does, and then see if that company is willing to give you even BIGGER rewards for building a NETWORK of people who are buying that product.

8. Here is a really puzzling thing about money – almost everyone who does NOT have money is going to tell you that you are crazy.

9. Think about this: People who do not have enough money *usually* do not have enough money for a reason.

10. Finally, let me say this: *money has no memory.* If you did not make much money yesterday, money does not care. Don't worry about the past, worry about the future!

More About Sunny

Life can be tough. Sometimes, life can be downright tragic! You can have all kinds of bad things happen to you and to the people you love. Sickness, accidents, bad luck – it can all happen. When it does, you can get depressed. If you are depressed, get some help from a trained person.

But, there are also many wonderful things about life, and it is your job to make sure you take advantage of every opportunity to maintain that "Sunny" outlook. Be aware and awake. Participate in life to the fullest. Help others participate in all the positive, exciting and satisfying things life has to offer.

I am always amazed when I see people who are just neglecting their basic health. Whether it is bad diets, bad decisions, bad habits, or bad judgement, you can really mess up an otherwise perfectly good life!

In this computer-driven, television-watching world of ours, it is sooooo easy to get out of shape. Inactivity is a terrible by product of our modern, convenient life.

Folks, you were given a human body. Take good care of it! I mean it – it is so easy to do SOMETHING. And, here is the best news, unlike money, (which has no memory) your body DOES have a memory. When you make simple, small changes to your diet or exercise routine, you are building up *memory* in your body. For example, if you begin to simply *walk* a mile every other day, your body will remember it, and will send you signals, telling you if you forget to take that walk one day. Get in tune with your body, and LISTEN to it.

The same thing can be said about simply maintaining a positive, mental and spiritual outlook on life. One of the key elements to becoming positive is to get around positive people, but the most important thing about being positive and optimistic (key elements in a Sunny attitude) is to actually take positive steps towards achieving your dream! Read positive books. Speak to positive people. Join a business that has positive values and attitudes, and a positive plan for your future.

More About Honey

If you want to have great relationships with others, you need to become the kind of person that other people like being around. This is part of the "Law of Attractions." Be attractive!

I love to fish, and I have learned quite a bit about life through fishing. When I go fishing, I am making a positive decision to attract fish! I mean ... I want LOTS of fish around me when I am fishing. Doesn't that make sense?

But, when I am fishing, I want to attract the right kind of fish. I have some *target* species. For example, I LOVE Mahi Mahi. Not only are they fun to catch, they taste great. I love eating fish, because it is healthier than eating red meat. (Go back to Sunny!)

Where do I fish for Mahi Mahi? I fish for them where they live! I go to the "Mahi Mahi" spots, because I am more likely to catch Mahi there, and LESS likely to catch other kinds of fish there. (I am not targeting fish that don't taste great – just fish that I like to eat. I don't want to catch other kinds of fish.)

What kinds of bait do I use for Mahi? I use the kinds of bait they already like to eat. I don't try to convince the Mahi to eat something they don't want to eat. I don't try to tell them "Hey Mahi, you guys really need to change your ways and eat this, instead of the things you like to eat."

When do I fish for Mahi? ALL THE TIME! Why? Because I never know when they will be biting, so if I fish for them all the time, I will be there when THEY are ready to eat.

People Aren't Mahi, but...

Now, when I am trying to build positive relationships, with positive people, I do the things that positive people find attractive.

Where do I go to find positive people? I go to wherever positive people are already congregating. Do you know where I do not generally find positive people? I generally do not find them in bars! I find them in places where positive people go to be positive.

Who do you find sitting in bars? You find people who are kind of grumpy! They are just sitting there. (Hey, I'm not saying everyone sitting in a bar is a negative person. I am just saying that I like my chances better where there is positive energy.)

And, when I am looking to build relationships with positive people, I try to avoid people who are not my "target species." Who are these people? They are all the people who are constantly complaining, or have lives full of self-generated drama, or just can't seem to get excited about anything positive.

Think about this, when you go fishing, you hardly ever catch fish that don't like your bait.

Okay, now maybe you didn't like the fishing analogy, but let's face it. I am writing a book on dream building. I am telling you lots of positive stuff. But, I would not be doing my best if I didn't point out the BIG truths in life. I you are serious about developing positive, rewarding relationships, you have to realize that the only way to do that is to find positive people to have the relationships with!

Go Ahead, Rate My Day!

In the next chapter, I am going to call on Clint Eastwood's Character, Dirty Harry. (Yes, I know, not the most positive of people!)

Dirty Harry has a great line in the movie. He tells the bad guy (who is about to attack him), "Go ahead. Make my Day" Well, I am going to show you how to Rate YOUR Day – every day. It is a fantastic way to determine how much progress you made on the three super-variables of Money, Sunny and Honey, and just as importantly, it will end each and every day of your life on a positive note.

CHAPTER 15

Rate My Day

Okay, let's look at where we were, where we are, and where we are going. This is great stuff. I am having a blast writing this, and I hope you are seeing just how powerful Dream-Building is, and why it is so important for a successful, happy life.

1. We talked about the difference between being half asleep, and being Wide Awake when it comes to creating motivating, powerful, success-driving Dreams.

2. We discussed the difference between "looking back" with Maslow, as opposed to looking ahead with positive, Wide Awake Dreams.

3. I showed you how to categorize and prioritize your Dreams, right? You learned how to do "checklist analysis."

4. In the last chapter, I showed you three super-dream categories: Money, Sunny and Honey. We even spent some time talking about each of these three categories, and why they are important to your success.

Now, it's time to take the LAST STEP in the process – setting up a system to *evaluate your performance* in reaching your Dreams. In this chapter, you are going to get that system, and then I am going to show you how to do it every day, for the rest of your life! But, best of all, I am going to share a secret with you. You can actually Rate Your Day, in just a few minutes each day. And – get this – when you do, you will actually be able to get a better night's sleep!

Wow, could anything be better?

A Better Night's Sleep

Let's start with the BIG REWARD first. Sleep is important. If you are not getting enough sleep every night, you can't be Wide Awake in the daytime. Something has to give when you are tired, and usually, the first thing to get dropped is your Dreams! Remember, you have to be Wide Awake when you build Dreams.

So, why aren't you getting enough sleep? Well, for most people, *getting* to sleep is difficult, especially if you are under stress. You lie down, put your head on the pillow, and then start worrying about all the things you didn't get done that day – or all the things that are facing you in the morning.

Does that happen to you? Do you go to bed, exhausted from working and worrying all day, and then you lie there, unable to get to sleep, because you are worried about all kinds of things. After a few minutes, you add another worry to your already stressed-out mind. What is the NEW worry? You are worried that you can't fall asleep, and you have a big day ahead of you. "Why can't I simply shut down my mind? I am so worried about not getting enough sleep. What time is now? Oh no, I have been lying here awake for an hour. That's an hour less sleep! I am going to be worthless tomorrow!"

You know how this goes, right? Well, what if I can show you a way to get rid of many of the worries you have so you can get to sleep? Would that help you out? I'm sure it would.

Look, the system I am about to show you might take some time to get used to. I mean… you have been living without enough sleep for *years*. You have been having trouble falling asleep for *years*. Don't think you can change overnight! It will take some work. But, the results are worth it. Believe me. I know!

The Big Secret

The big secret to shutting off your mind, and peacefully falling asleep, is to separate your day job from your night job. That's right. You need to *quit* your day job for eight hours – and not worry about it – so you can go to your night job – sleeping and recovering. It's that simple.

So, how exactly do you do that? How do you shut down your day job, and clock in for your night job? Simple. You do a daily evaluation of your day job's effectiveness, and then make a conscious decision to put off any more worrying, thinking, fretting, or stressing, until you wake up!

And, I am going to give you a simple tool – a simple technique – so that you can clock out of one job, and clock in on another.

But Bill, You Don't Seem To Like Jobs!

For most jobs, you trade time for dollars. The more dollars you want to earn, the more time you put into it.

But, let's face it. Almost everyone has a job. They do pay money! They do help you pay your bills. But, you have to know when they STOP paying you money in order to succeed.

For example, let's say you work in a restaurant. You go in and work your shift. When your restaurant closes for the day, you CAN'T make any more money, right? RIGHT! So, you should KNOW this. When you can't make money, stop working, because it just doesn't pay.

But, maybe you have other "jobs" in your life. Maybe you go to the gym to work out, so that you will be healthier (Sunny), or maybe you have kids, and a spouse, so you want to spend time with them and build your relationships with them. (Honey) In a sense, the *Sunny* and *Honey* parts of your life are like a job. If you work at them, they produce results. Work on your Sunny by exercising, and you build health. Work on your Honey by spending quality time with your kids and your spouse, and you build your relationships.

But, if you go to bed, but can't sleep because you are thinking about the exercise you MISSED today, that doesn't pay off at all, right? And if you go to bed, and think about the fight you had with your kids, or how your spouse isn't communicating with you, THAT isn't paying off either, is it? It is the same as serving tables and cooking food, *after the restaurant has closed!* There is simply no profit in it. You are working on a job, but there is no job. You are just wasting sleep time – time that could be used for something else – like rebuilding your shattered nerves, or relaxing you so you can get up early the next day, be Wide Awake, and make a difference – at a time when doing your Money, Sunny, or Honey-producing job actually makes sense.

So, How Do You Shut Down Your Day Jobs?

What are you thinking about, stressing about, or worrying about at night? Well, it is probably something from the Money, Sunny or Honey super variables that you identified in your Checklist Analysis. Here are some examples:

Money – You didn't get that report done at work. Your boss is going to be angry. Maybe you didn't call a customer back. It's driving you crazy.

Sunny – You ate three doughnuts for dessert tonight. You are feeling guilty, because you really wanted to lose some weight so you would look good in your bathing suit this summer. Oh wait… NOW you remember what you looked like last year, and summer starts in a week!

Honey – You lost your temper with one of your kids today. Of course, if he had just listened to you, that _____ would not have broken! (Fill in that blank!) Why did you let him get under your skin like that? You know it always happens.

Aren't these the kind of things that you lie awake and think about? I can tell you that I do! Sometimes, I go over the things that went wrong during the day, or the things I forgot to do, or did wrong. It drives me crazy, and robs me of much needed sleep.

So, What Is Your Problem?

Well, I already mentioned that you are not separating your day jobs from your night job. But, there is more to it than that. The problem that most people have is that they never *end their day job shifts*. They don't do a "wrap up," so they never end their day jobs. Here is what you have to do to change all that:

1. Do a Rate My Day evaluation for Money, Sunny and Honey.
2. Make a quick mental list of the things you did today that had a positive impact on your life, in all three categories.
3. Set some quick goals for tomorrow, in all three categories.
4. Then, *forget about it!* At this point, you can shut down your mind, and let it all go. You either did a good job today (on your day jobs) or you didn't. NOTHING you do on your night job is going to change that. If you didn't make a few contact calls (Money), you can't make them while you (and they) are sleeping! If it is midnight, a contact call is probably not going to be received favorably by your prospect – especially if he is in the same time zone. If you DIDN'T make enough contact calls today, give yourself a bad grade for your Money today, and then set some goals for tomorrow. Say to yourself, "I didn't make ANY contact calls today. That was bad. That is no way to achieve my dream of owning a big house on the lake within five years. Tomorrow, I am going to make three contact calls."

HINT: Maybe you want to keep a small diary next to your bed, so that you can write down your goals. Or, just send yourself a text message, with your "make three contact calls tomorrow" goal on the text.

BIG HINT: DO NOT try to make up any things you didn't do today, by doubling down tomorrow. For example, if you were supposed to make three contact calls today, and you DIDN'T make them, DO NOT say, "I will do SIX contact calls tomorrow." That almost NEVER works, and you know what it will do? It will make you start worrying, as soon as you lay your head on the pillow, and you will not get to sleep.

HINT: Treat your Money, Sunny and Honey day jobs just like you would treat a job in a restaurant. When the place closes, stop working!

One Day at a Time

I was in the Hotel business for quite some time in my life. In fact, when I was just 19, I owned and operated a small hotel in Ocean City, New Jersey. I can tell you one thing about a hotel, they never close! A hotel is open 24 hours a day, 365 days per year (and an extra day in Leap Year.) Even if the restaurant in your hotel closes, if you have guests sleeping in your rooms, you are technically still open. In fact, there used to be a tradition in the hotel business, whenever a new hotel was opened. At the opening ceremony, the General Manager would unlock the front door, and then throw away the key. I can remember learning about this tradition during my first semester at the Hotel School at Cornell University, where I did my undergraduate work.

(Of course, they didn't throw away the ONLY key to the front door!)

But, even though the hotel was technically open all night, every hotel has a "business day" when the accounts are settled. For example, suppose the guest in room 101 is paying $200/night. At some point, that $200 is charged to the guest's account. And, if that guest had dinner in the restaurant, and charged it to the room, at some point, that charge is made, and the day's accounts are settled. In most hotels, the business day ended about 2 a.m. – which is after the restaurants and bar are closed. When the day ended, the hotel's accountant would "settle" the accounts, and charge any outstanding balances to the guests' bill.

Have You Thrown Away Your Front Door Key?

But, a LOT of people throw away their front door key, and NEVER settle the accounts. They never put some annoying, stressful or *looming* things into the "yesterday's work" file. They never settle their accounts for the day, and they carry the worries, stress, unfinished business, and all the other clutter, right through the night. They end up losing sleep, and they wake up stressed out, all because of what happened… YESTERDAY. This is terrible. Yesterday's business is closed. Why worry about it.

Just Close Your Accounts

Folks, it doesn't matter what you did or did not do yesterday. It is over. Set some goals, drop the guilt, and get on with it.

Let's go back to that "I didn't make contact calls." Forget it! Okay, you had a bad day. Close the books on it. Set your goals for tomorrow, "I will make 3 contact calls." When you wake up tomorrow, get busy. Did you feel bad last night when you did your Rate My Day exercise, and had to face up to the fact that you did not do what you intended to do in your Money job? Well, you SHOULD have felt bad about it. It was a let-down for your team! You said you were going to do it, but you didn't.

Hey, did the world end? Did your family fall apart? Probably not.

But, if you don't want to feel bad again TONIGHT, get busy and get those calls made. That way, when you go to bed TONIGHT, you will have a feeling of satisfaction. You will sleep better. You will LOOK better the next morning.

Rome Wasn't Built In a Day

Did you ever hear this expression? Roman myth has it that a set of twins, "Romulus and Remus" were raised by wolves, and that they built Rome on seven hills. Guess what? It didn't get done in a day. Do you think Romulus and Remus had big fights over how long it took to build Rome? Did Romulus say, "Hey Remus? I thought you were going to get hills six and seven all built today! What's with you? Are you stupid, or lazy?" And If Romulus DID say this, do you think that Remus thought, "Oh no. Twenty-four hours have passed, and I still haven't even built out hill one."

No, Rome wasn't built in a day, and you are not going to achieve your Dreams in a day either. Give yourself a break. Build a long-term plan, and work at it day-after-day, but not at night!

Back To Our Dreams...

When Jeanne and I set out our Dreams, I had not discovered the Money, Sunny and Honey variables yet, nor had I learned to use checklist analysis of prioritize my Dreams. But, we did make some great goals for ourselves, and I DID do a Rate My Day analysis each and every day. For example, one of the most meaningful (and liberating) goals I set for myself was, "Never let the sun set on a day when I didn't do *something* positive to help me reach my Dreams."

Folks, I tell you, this great goal was so simple, yet so powerful. It allowed me to do extraordinary things *at the last minute, at the very end of the day.* For example, I had a number of "Positive" things I could do. A "positive" thing might be as simple as spending 15 minutes reading an inspirational book. (Or, in my case, *writing* an inspirational book!). It might have been a short exercise period. In other words, my goal was to do SOMETHING positive before I laid down in bed, ready to sleep and take a big stab at doing something positive the next day.

Sure, there were some days when I really had to hustle to get something positive done before going to bed. But, I RARELY went to bed without that goal being reached.

And, if I just did a minimal amount of positive stuff in a day, I would say to myself, "Bill, you can do better tomorrow." I wouldn't beat myself up, or stress about it. I would shut down, and do better the next day.

Remember, Jeanne and I Took 5 Years to Achieve Our Dreams

We didn't build our Rome in a day. We were in it for the long term. At the time of this writing, we have been married for 34 years. We have good days and great days in our marriage. We work at it, but we don't stress over it, because we try to do something positive each day. We live in a fantastic house by the beach. We didn't get this house in a day. We bought it, and went to work to pay for it. We slowly upgraded and renovated the house. (In 2012, Super Storm Sandy *un-renovated* it, and we had to start over. We didn't do THAT in a day, I can tell you that!)

No Day Is Final – You Get Another One

Look, I understand that ONE OF THESE DAYS it is going to be the last day of your life. But, you are only going to get ONE of those days! Most people will get *thousands* of days. I can tell you I plan to wake up tomorrow, so if today isn't my very best day, I am going to get another shot at it tomorrow.

In other words, I Rate Each Day – not to single out that day, not to give each day so much importance. I Rate Each Day so that I can set better goals and standards for myself tomorrow – *if I need to do it!* Very rarely do I have a bad day in all three areas. If my Money wasn't my best effort today, chances are good that I hit it squarely in the middle with my Sunny or Honey.

Habits, Like Rome, Are Not Built In a Day

Look, this is all about building habits. Success is habit forming. So is failure. You need to develop good habits for success. It will take time, and you will always have days that didn't go as well as you would have liked them to go. That's okay – if you have good habits. With good habits, you can get back on track tomorrow.

Make It Easy

When you go to bed, just review your Money, Sunny and Honey. Be honest with yourself, but don't be brutal. If you think it will help you build habits, build a list. Write down a few things to review in each of the three categories. Give yourself a grade. Jot down a few goals for tomorrow, and remember, don't make them cumulative. (If you missed your number of contact calls today, don't add that number onto tomorrow's goal.)

Remember how good it feels to have made a positive difference in your life by doing something every day.

And NEVER work after the restaurant closes. It never pays off!

CHAPTER 16
Happy Anniversary

Here is something very special that I wanted to share with you, my reader. Today is July 7, 2018. It is *exactly* 2:30 in the afternoon, EDT. Do you know what that means? Can you think of any other date that I gave you in this book?

How about July 7, 1993, at 2:30 in the afternoon?

Yep… it is exactly 25 years since I saw those people laughing on the stern of that yacht in Fort Lauderdale! It is the Silver Anniversary of my Alarm going off – and exactly 25 years since I told my wife, Jeanne, that I wanted to change our lives.

Today, however, I am sitting in front of my computer, in my home on a barrier island off New Jersey. Our home is a beautiful Victorian-style house that we purchased in July, 2003 – exactly 15 years ago. It is right off the beach. This morning, I took a walk on the boardwalk. I love this place!

How did we end up here? It was simple, but not easy. Remember, on July 7, 1993, we were living *inland*, in Orlando, Florida. Within 5 years, we had moved to that little island off Miami Beach. We purchased the New Jersey beach home in 2003, as an income-producing property. In 2005, we moved here full time, so that our daughters could go to the beachside high school, right across the street. The high school here is excellent, and we wanted to give our daughters the best opportunity to launch their lives.

We were able to do all these things because of one thing – *we woke up, after hearing the alarm, 25 years ago*. It hasn't always been easy. For example, my business really suffered during the recession in 2008. I had to go back to work as a college professor, while we rebuilt our businesses, and rebuilt our financial position. But, it paid off. We kept our lifestyle, and today, as I write these words, we are once again prosperous.

It Was The Dream That Made The Difference

Folks, I owe all of the success over the last 25 years to one thing – I had a clear, vivid, compelling Dream. My wife shared that Dream with me. We always knew exactly what we wanted our lives to be like. We kept that picture of our Dream in front of us at all times. We also kept the pictures on the refrigerator, and later, on our smart phones.

You see, after the Alarm went off in 1993, I learned how to turn my Dreams into reality. I learned the secrets of making money, leveraging my time, building a network of like-minded people, and *filling the pipeline.*

When that recession hit in 2008, I didn't panic. I didn't revert to a Maslow-like method of thinking. Yes, I hustled and focused on making money to cover our immediate expenses, but even during the worst of that Recession, both Jeanne and I kept our *Wide Awake, Motivational-Dream-Focus on our Dreams.* We didn't lose sight of what our life *should* be, even though our situation had changed. We didn't lose our sense of humor, or our optimism, just because things got rough. We had tasted real freedom in our lives, and we were determined not just to survive the Recession, but to rebuild our lifestyle and gain back our freedom.

Today, we are still on that journey. Truthfully, we are not back 100% to where we were in late 2008. But, we are in so much better shape than we were in early 2009!

Today, I am in my sixties. My financial situation is excellent – *and getting better each month!* (How many people my age can say that?) We have two homes in Florida, and are looking at more.

As for relationships, we just celebrated our 34th wedding anniversary. Our oldest daughter is getting married next week, and guess what? We are still speaking to each other! (No Bride-zilla.) Our younger daughter is a restaurant manager nearby, and she is still speaking to us! (And even picks up part of our tab when we stop in her restaurant.)

We have a wonderful group of friends. Each of them contributes to our life in meaningful ways, and they are all forward-looking, Dream-building people. We chose, 25 years ago – to associate with positive people. We never regretted that decision.

A Proud Moment – A Dream Fulfilled

Way back in 1993, when Jeanne and I first built our Dreams, we made one promise that we kept. One of our Dreams was to pay for our children's education, through their college degrees. We didn't want them to suffer from crushing student debt when they graduated. I am happy, and proud, to say that neither child has ANY student debt. One graduated from college in 2013, and the other in 2016. Many of their classmates owe thousands of dollars.

Now, I have to tell you this – Jeanne and I owe money on our daughters' education. In our original Dream plan, we would simply pay for their college tuitions out of our income and savings. And, *some* of their tuition money came out of our "cash-on-hand" funds. But, after that Recession, we had to take out some loans to pay for the tuition. Hey, it happens! But again, we didn't panic, and we took out student loans in our name, while we continued to rebuild our businesses. Today, we are rapidly paying off that debt. We are using income we generated by filling our pipelines.

Sometimes, we have to make adjustments. If you build a Dream, and dedicate your time and energy towards achieving that Dream, you can make the adjustments, and still get everything you want.

What's Next?

Here's the exciting answer to the question, "What's Next?" No one knows. I certainly don't know. I know what we have *planned*, but after all the challenges and ever-changing situations that life has dealt me, I also know that none of us can guarantee anything in this life. Health can change. Finances can change. Relationships can change. (I call them Money, Sunny and Honey.) There could be another massive Recession. Technology could change, and some of my businesses could be put out of business. One of us could get sick, or die. We just don't know.

All we can do is to make certain that we are as ready as we can be for uncertainty. We live strong – strong in determination, faith and healthy practices.

On The Other Hand...

On the other hand, we DO know some things for certain. We live in the United States. We are free to make our best choices – or our worst ones. We are certain that Good is Good, and Evil is Evil. We know that, in the coming years, NO ONE is going to give us anything. NO ONE is going to have our best interests at heart – except for those closest to us. NO ONE is going to give us money, or pay our bills, or take us on vacations, or provide for our Dreams – except us. And, we know that one day, it won't be an "us" anymore.

We also know that NO ONE ELSE is going to teach our children to live strong and free. And, even though our children are now adults, we know for certain that we must *continue* to teach them, through example, that there is a different way to live – a way to live with freedom and dignity – if you only Wake Up and Dream.

What Do You Know Now, And What Will YOU Know In 25 Years?

Okay, you are probably younger than I am – maybe MUCH younger. But, after reading this book, what do you know? Hopefully, you know what I do. Hopefully, you can see just how crazy our educational system has become. Hopefully, you can see how crazy the promises of politicians, bosses, brothers-in-law, and even well-meaning friends and family can be. And hopefully, you can see how to change all that so that you can live free.

I am confident, if you have read this book carefully, you now know how to build a Dream, and then fulfill that Dream, no matter what challenges life sends your way. You now know that you can have a lifestyle that is completely different than the one that your current friends and family have. It is definitely within your grasp.

And, as I sit here writing, on the 25th anniversary of WAKING UP and DREAMING in my own life, I hope that you realize the satisfaction I feel as I look *back* on those 25 years.

Here Is What I Hope You Never Know

Folks, for all of you, I hope you never know the disappointment of looking back on 25 years of your life, and thinking, "I should have done this differently." And, I am not talking about things like, "I should have saved more money out of my paycheck." EVERYONE wishes they had saved more money! That's a given!

No, I am talking about the feeling that I know for certain many people do have in this world. They look back on 25 years, and say, "Where did that time go? What am I going to do now?"

Look, in the next 25 years, you know for certain that you are going to either live, or die. (Actually, some of you might do both!) So do this: live free! Look down at your leg. There is nothing there that is tying you to the stake in the ground. No one is stopping you from Waking Up right now, and staying awake for the rest of your life – however long or short that might be.

And, if you do make it another 25 years, I want you to have the satisfaction of saying, "Wow, I did G-R-E-A-T! I am so proud."

Because I can tell you this one thing. It does fell G-R-E-A-T!

Wake Up and Dream – for a lifetime.